the mediterranean REFRESH

the mediterranean REFRESH

Erika Simons

peapil

PEAPIL PUBLISHING
PO Box 65460
Salt Lake City, Utah 84165
www.peapil.com

Designed by Ashley Tucker
Cover Design by Ashley Tucker

Third Edition

Contact the author at support@peapil.com
Paperback ISBN: 978-1-9995720-6-8
eBook ISBN: 978-1-9995720-8-2

Disclaimer
All material on Peapil.com and in this book is provided for your information only and may not be construed as medical advice or instruction. No action or inaction should be taken based solely on the contents of this information; instead, readers should consult appropriate health professionals on any matter relating to their health and well-being. If you think you may have a medical emergency, call your doctor or 911 immediately.

The content of this book (text, graphics and images) is not intended to be a substitute for professional medical advice, diagnosis or treatment. Always seek the advice of your physician or other qualified health provider with any questions you may have regarding a medical condition.

Never disregard professional medical advice or delay in seeking it because of something you have read in this book. The information and opinions expressed here are believed to be accurate, based on the best judgment available to the authors. Readers who fail to consult with appropriate health authorities assume the risk of any injuries. Reliance on any information and content provided by Peapil Publishing and this book is solely at your own risk.

The publisher is not responsible for errors or omissions.

Rev 3.0

CONTENTS

Introduction to the Mediterranean Lifestyle

I know … I know… It's called the Mediterranean Diet. But I hate that word *diet.* It sounds like you're going to have to stop eating all your favorite foods, start calorie counting or join some cultlike exercise place—the word's been used for decades to describe some pretty horrific things.

But have no fear.

This book isn't about dieting, calorie counting or anything like that. It's about adopting a lifestyle that's been around for hundreds of years: a lifestyle full of delicious, seasonal and fresh foods. The Mediterranean Diet is full of an unlimited amount of food from all nutritional groups. Although the focus may be on foods that you're not familiar with, no food groups are completely excluded. There are no hard-and-fast rules—just "less of this" and "more of that" guidelines.

The diet is based on the eating habits of people on the coasts of Italy, Morocco, Spain, Greece and France. People living on the shores of the Mediterranean have a very healthy diet because of the abundance of heart-healthy foods found right outside their doors: foods like fresh fish, nuts and fruit. Imagine going on a Mediterranean vacation—you get to eat like this every day. Including, yes, a little bit of wine!

This isn't the typical restrictive North American "diet."

The Mediterranean Diet is widely acknowledged to be one of the healthiest diets in the world, and one of the most delicious as well, bar none.

> "But the benefits of the Mediterranean Diet don't only happen as you age. You'll notice (and feel) some of the changes almost immediately."

People in the Mediterranean (at least, those who haven't succumbed to a McDonald's-heavy diet) have a reduced risk of heart disease. The Mediterranean Diet is associated with a lower level of oxidized low-density lipoprotein (LDL) cholesterol. This is the "bad" cholesterol that is likely to build up deposits in your arteries.

A study of nearly 26,000 women found that those who followed this type of diet had 25 percent less risk of developing cardiovascular disease over the course of 12 years.[1] This means they were less likely to die from heart-related diseases and lived longer over a total period of time. Following the guidelines of a Mediterranean Diet resulted in lower levels of inflammation, lower blood sugar and a lower body mass index—all of which are the primary drivers of increased heart disease risk when their respective levels are too high.

One myth that these studies has debunked is the idea that eating "low-fat" foods can reduce the risk of heart disease. As you'll discover, the Mediterranean Diet actually encourages eating fats—but these are good-for-you fats. That means lots of extra-virgin olive oil and nuts. The risk of diabetes is also decreased by eating Mediterranean foods.[2]

Eating more olive oil and mixed nuts has also been shown to reduce the risk of breast cancer, and the healthy fats you get from the Mediterranean Diet have been linked to a decreased likelihood of other cancers, Parkinson's disease and even Alzheimer's disease. The same study also found that women who followed the Mediterranean Diet were 46 percent more likely to age healthfully. Eating plants, whole grains and fish, and even drinking a bit of red wine—plus skipping processed foods—are a great way to get past 70 years old without developing chronic diseases or declines in mental health.[3]

Getting plenty of fresh foods, healthy fats and natural sugars—as opposed to our typical processed, artificial, sugar-choked diet—leads to a longer, more productive life with less fear of mental and physical illnesses in the future.

The Mediterranean Diet has been recommended by the American Heart Association as a great way to try and prevent cardiac diseases.[4] And that's one of the primary reasons it has become so popular.

But the benefits of the Mediterranean Diet don't only happen as you age. You'll notice (and feel) some of the changes almost immediately.

Immediate Benefits of the Mediterranean Diet

- Detoxed liver and colon
- Curbed sugar cravings
- Boosted energy levels
- Ease in maintaining an ideal weight
- Less inflammation
- Easier blood sugar management

Why I Got Involved

My name is **Erika Simons**, and I'm currently the head recipe coach over at *Mediterranean Refresh*! I joined the team there because it was created specifically for people like me and you who want to transform our bodies and lives.

I'm a mother and a daughter who has firsthand experience with the disastrous results of our processed, unnatural, sugar-filled lifestyles.

I wouldn't be the woman I am today if it weren't for my mother. I owe her so much. I'm sure many of you can relate.

My mother was an incredible chef who trained under some of the best culinary minds in California, and she taught me everything she knew about cooking. By the time I was a teenager, she had shown me how to make authentic dishes from places like Japan, Italy, Greece and so many others.

> "Healthy cooking became the key to unlocking my best life possible."

The only trouble was, even though my mom could create meals that people happily paid hundreds of dollars for, she struggled with her weight and, more important, her health.

As a young girl, I watched her battle with an eating disorder. While my family and I would eat the incredible dinners she cooked for us, she seemed only to push food around her plate with a fork, never taking a bite.

That is, until I turned 14, and everything changed.

This was the year my mom was put in the hospital for the first time. Her dietary habits were unsustainable, and her body didn't know what to make of the food she was eating. She was never able to bring herself to eat the kinds of foods that would properly nourish her, and it took a severe toll on her health and our entire family.

So, for months at a time, we would visit her in the hospital. Over the span of three years her health rapidly declined, until she passed away in May 2003.

It was at this point, after the loss of my mother, that I decided to take a stand and change my life by turning away from the standard American diet.

I made up my mind I would never again eat anything that could threaten my chance to be around my children for as long as possible. I was tired of being tired, overweight and headed down the same path as my mom.

From that point forward, healthy cooking became the key to unlocking my best possible life. After reading about the problems caused by our typical diet, I became obsessed. Surely, the longevity of a particular country indicates how good its overall diet is, so I started researching different cultures. Which ones had the lowest rates of heart disease, Alzheimer's and Parkinson's? Where were the people naturally lean and energetic?

During my hunt I discovered dozens of cultures where people have longer lives and less illness. It's true: our diets affect our lives more than we care to admit.

But there was a problem. So many of these "healthy" diets were based on restrictive eating—eating small amounts of bland, tasteless food. As a recipe developer, I consider delicious food an essential part of life.

If you told me I'd live longer if I chose not to be a mother, I would tell you to get lost. A short life full of joy is better than a long one. While diet may be a less extreme example than having children, the same philosophy remains true. I *need* to eat delicious food. I'd rather die than be stuck with bland, tasteless food all my life. It's just part of my soul.

That's when I stumbled on the Mediterranean Diet. My research indicated that it was in fact one of the best choices in the world based on

longevity and reduced incidence of disease. And when I explored the diet in greater depth, I discovered just how delicious the food can be.

I decided to give it a shot.

I didn't have any recipes and had no idea how to get started. But little by little, I started to feel a lot better.

I felt refreshed ... energized! I was sleeping more easily, and I had zero brain fog in the morning. After just a couple of weeks, I started spending more time with my children again. I was even more active at work!

It took months, but I eventually developed a whole catalog of recipes to choose from. I started adapting my favorite American recipes to fit into the Mediterranean Diet. I altered traditional Mediterranean recipes to make them easier to make. I only chose ingredients I could find at the local supermarket.

In time, I became really proficient as a Mediterranean chef, and my friends and family started asking me constantly for healthy recipes. Every day, I see how the recipes I adapt and create are changing lives. My friends and family all have slimmer waistlines and higher energy, sleep more deeply and feel better overall.

But friends and family kept asking me for the recipes. And after a while, I got tired of continually writing out each one. So I started looking into publishing, and that's when I bumped into the Peapil Publishing team. They worked with me to help develop the wonderful recipes you see in this book today. All of these recipes are approved for the Mediterranean Diet and contain no artificial ingredients.

1. Ahmad S, Moorthy MV, Demler OV, Hu FB, Ridker PM, Chasman DI, and Mora S. "Assessment of Risk Factors and Biomarkers Associated with Risk of Cardiovascular Disease Among Women Consuming a Mediterranean Diet." *JAMA Network Open*. 2018

2. Salas-Salvadó J, Bulló M, Babio N, Martínez-González MÁ, Ibarrola-Jurado N, Basora J, Estruch R, Covas MI, Corella D, Arós F, and Ruiz-Gutiérrez V. "Reduction in the incidence of type 2 diabetes with the Mediterranean diet." *Diabetes care*. 2011

3. Samieri C, Sun Q, Townsend MK, Chiuve SE, Okereke OI, Willett WC, Stampfer M, and Grodstein F. "The Association Between Dietary Patterns at Midlife and Health in Aging: An Observational Study." *Annals of internal medicine*. 2013

4. Mediterranean Diet. www.heart.org. https://www.heart.org/en/healthy-living/healthy-eating/eat-smart/nutrition-basics/mediterranean-diet. Published 2019. Accessed January 14, 2019.

Essential Elements of the Mediterranean Diet

In a nutshell, the Mayo Clinic emphasizes three major points about the Mediterranean Diet:

1. Eating primarily plant-based foods, such as fruits and vegetables, whole grains, legumes and nuts

2. Replacing butter with healthy fats such as olive oil and canola oil; and

3. Using herbs and spices instead of salt to flavor foods.

Note that the diet doesn't require eliminating fat from your diet. Many trending food lifestyles like keto and paleo actually recommend fat, and this diet is no different. It's overall a less restrictive diet that believes in fresh foods, whole grains and legumes.

Use Olive Oil

Olive oil is the primary source of fat in this diet. It provides monounsaturated fat—a type that reduces LDL (bad) cholesterol levels. We recommend extra-virgin olive oil because it has the highest levels of the plant compounds that actually provide antioxidant effects.

Recent research indicates that olive oil protects against chronic diseases and helps in the battle against diabetes, obesity and cancer. Owing to its cardioprotective role, it provides antihypertensive, antithrombotic, antioxidant, anti-inflammatory and anticarcinogenic action.

The diet isn't about limiting total fat consumption, but rather making good choices about which fats to consume. To enjoy the diet's fullest benefits, avoid saturated fats and hydrogenated oils, which contain trans fats. These unhealthy fats are tied to heart disease and will counteract all the healing that your body is otherwise undergoing.

"One of the best parts of this diet is hitting up the local farmer's markets and choosing what to eat based on the seasons."

Eat Fish

Even if you're not a fish lover, there are plenty of delicious recipes to experiment with. Fish is a rich source of omega-3 fatty acids.

The fish in this diet is cooked fresh and is never deep-fried. Don't worry, there are plenty of directions in the recipe section of this book.

Enjoy Wine Time

The health effects of wine have been debated forever, but most experts agree that as long as you don't drink excessively, wine can be a wonderful component of a healthy diet. If you choose to drink wine, we recommend limiting your consumption to 5 ounces per day for those over the age of 65 and 10 ounces per day for those under 65.

Go Nuts

Nuts are another vital food group in the diet. They contain beneficial linolenic acid (a type of omega-3 fatty acid). Omega-3 fatty acids lower triglycerides, decrease blood clotting and may lower risk of sudden heart attack, improve the health of your blood vessels and help moderate blood pressure.

Nuts are high in fat, but most of the fat is not saturated. Make sure not to eat too many, about a handful a day. Also avoid corner-store candied nuts. I recommend unsalted nuts and love fresh walnuts, pistachios and almonds. Cashews are also a tasty choice.

Replacing your regular snacks with fresh nuts is a great way to reduce empty calories and avoid added sugar and sodium. Nuts are also a great source of fiber and minerals like potassium, which makes them a much better choice than processed snack foods.

Eat Veggies and Fruit

Make sure to always include a handful of veggies with every dish you prepare. Don't be afraid to serve a piece of fruit for desert or add it to a recipe for an extra bit of natural sweetness. In general, always pick fresh fruit over processed sugar. One of the best parts of this diet is hitting up the local farmer's markets and choosing what to eat based on the season's offerings. I've found it's a wonderful way to educate my children, and they love going!

A good rule of thumb: eat veggies all day long, with every meal. It's simply the best way to get extra nutrients and fill your tummy without a ton of calories, and veggies have actually been proven to reduce stress.

Fruits are the best way to satisfy your sweet tooth. Because fruit contains fiber and the sugar is naturally occurring, it won't spike your blood sugar nearly as much as the same amount of added sugar would. Full of vitamin C and antioxidants, fruits are a great way to complete a well-balanced diet.

Switch to Whole Grains

This is such a simple way to increase the amount of fiber and nutrition in your diet. I always recommend whole grains for a delicious guilt-free pasta dish.

Ingredients used in the Mediterranean region are typically made from whole grains and contain very few trans fats. Bread is important to the diet but is never served with butter or margarine. We avoid these because they contain trans fats.

Eat Less Red Meat

Substitute fish and poultry for red meat. When you do choose red meat, try to make the portions small. And always opt for fresh meat over preserved or processed meats like sausage and jerky.

Choose Low-Fat, No-Sugar Dairy

We recommend low-fat yogurt with no added sugar. It's an easy way to get all the benefits of dairy without the baggage.

Add Spices

Spices are full of nutrients and anti-inflammatory properties—not to mention they can make any dish ten times more delicious. When going through the recipes, take note of which spices and herbs we recommend. Try to get good at knowing how much you like to add, and which ones are your favorite. Using spices wisely can help you reduce the amount of added sugar you need in your recipes.

Tips for Success

Before you get started on the Mediterranean Diet, it's a good idea to do a little bit of preparation. Oftentimes when we jump right into things, it's easy to become overwhelmed. So read on a bit and familiarize yourself with some of the basic principles before jumping into the recipes. Unless, of course, you just need something fun to eat—then feel free to pick an inviting recipe and get started!

Adapt Your Current Diet

Before jumping into the diet completely, take a quick look at what you currently enjoy and try to make subtle changes. Reduce the amount of red meat. Start cooking with olive oil. Try switching to low-fat yogurt. Decrease the number of sugary treats. Try to morph your current menus into the Mediterranean Diet instead of starting from scratch. Slowly moving toward this diet will make it harder to go back to less desirable habits.

Learn to make some simple substitutions. Instead of consuming a bag of chips, grab a fistful of nuts. Find something in the Mediterranean Diet that will make a healthy replacement for some of your less beneficial choices.

I've included whole sections on snack foods, drinks and even desserts to help you on your path. Take a look at those sections right now and think about which recipes would be a great substitute for some of the things you're eating now.

Your New Food Pyramid

This food pyramid was developed by The Mediterranean Diet Foundation Expert Group and shows which foods you should eat as part of the diet. Each recipe in this book closely follows this pyramid.

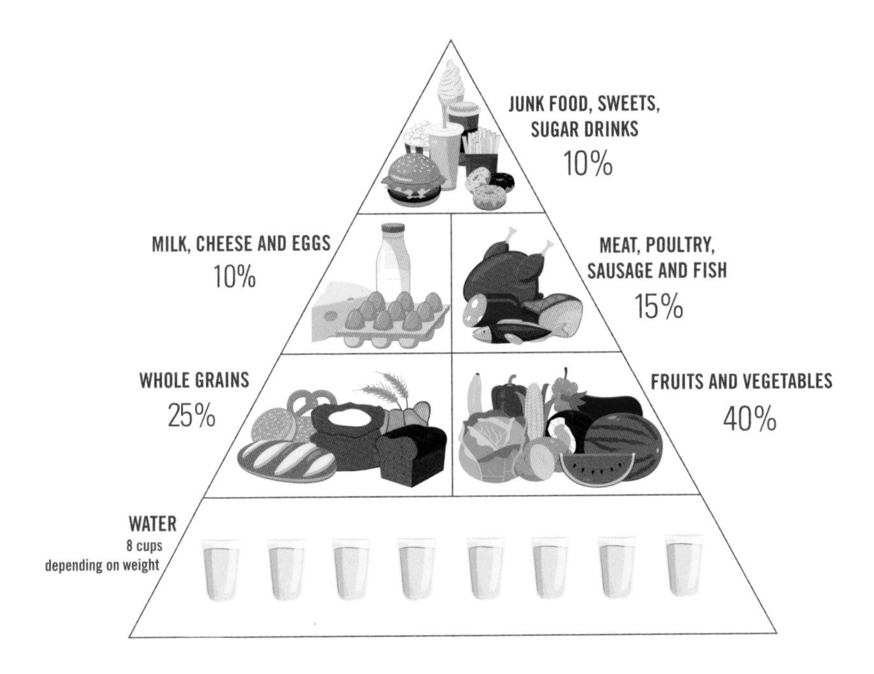

Here are the basic percentages of each food group you should aim for each day, based on the Mediterranean Food Pyramid:

Water	7-8 cups a day (8-oz)
Fresh Fruits and Vegetables	40% • Try to opt for fresh, seasonal fruits and veggies. If you're ever hungry, just know you can eat more veggies!
Whole Grains	25%
Dairy Products	10%
Meat, Poultry and Fish	15% • Always choose poultry over red meat. If serving red meat, make portions small.
Junk Food and Sweets	10%

The Pantry

In order to maintain the diet, it's important to stock up on the ingredients that are used in most of these recipes. It's always a good idea to have lots of fruits, vegetables, and nuts on hand as they go well in each Mediterranean dish. That way you're not running to the grocery store every day! I made sure each recipe in this book uses common ingredients, so you won't have to trek to specialty shops to try to find an obscure ingredient for a single recipe. No special equipment or appliances are needed.

And don't leave temptations in sight! Everything you buy at the grocery store will end up in your stomach... so just leave the bag of chips at the store. It's so much harder to avoid indulgence when the food is right there, waiting to be devoured. How often have you heard yourself say, "I wouldn't eat this, but it's going to go bad... so I have to!" It happens to me all the time.

Take a good look at your pantry and fridge. Review the information on pages 15–19, and try to give away or toss out ingredients such as your less healthy oils and margarine. I know it can be hard, and it may seem like a big waste of money. But the benefits of making a clean switch to this healthier way of living are way more valuable than the unhealthy food you need to get rid of.

Enjoy the Vacation

Take your time. Remember when I said the Mediterranean Diet is like eating as if you're on vacation? One of the core tenets of the diet is to take things slowly when dining. Instead of shoving food down as quickly as possible after going through a drive-through or mindlessly eating while watching Netflix, we invite you to sit down at the table with your family and friends. Slowly enjoy and savor what you're eating.

Gathering with friends and family and enjoying a freshly made meal is a vital part of the Mediterranean culture. Taking the time to share a meal with your loved ones, talking about the day and enjoying one another's presence, is an amazing experience.

Not only will you enjoy the food better but eating slowly allows you to pay attention to your stomach. It's good to get an awareness of when you're truly full to prevent overeating. Consuming smaller portion sizes is the easiest way to reduce weight, so be prepared to stop eating when you're satisfied. So often we end up eating until we need to start undoing our belts! Really pay attention while you eat slowly—take notes on what changes you'd like to make to a particular recipe in the future.

Exercise (Argh!)

No lifestyle book is complete without a little side note about exercise. Thankfully, if you go to our online community, you'll find dozens of resources that will help people just like you get into a more active lifestyle. I invite you to visit our community today!

Peapil.com

Try to get about 20 minutes of exercise every day. One "cheat" I use is to always take the stairs. I also make sure to park far away from the entrance when I go to the grocery store.

Little things like this force you to get a bit of exercise in. I've also tried to get more involved with my daughter's activities. Instead of sending her to dance class, I actually joined a mom-daughter class so we can work out together! It's so much more fun than just watching her dance, and I get to learn along with her and get some exercise at the same time!

How to Eat Out

When eating out, take care to pick a place where you're sure to get fresh instead of fried food. If you do happen to slip up and order fast food, don't beat yourself up. Even though I'm a full-time recipe developer, I sometimes end up with a sloppy burger in my hands! It's not going to kill you ... just make sure you don't make it a habit.

Lean more toward seafood places, farm-to-table food and Italian, Spanish and Greek restaurants. Vegetarian places are also a great choice! That said, most restaurants have plenty of Mediterranean-style options.

Avoid anything fried, and make sure to ask if you're not sure. Choose from the poultry or vegetarian options. Beef dishes are typically the most calorie-laden. Be very careful with sauces and dressings. I typically ask for mine to be served on the side. Try to avoid creamy sauces and ask for vinaigrette instead.

Most restaurants are used to substitutions for dietary restrictions, so don't be afraid to tell them what you're unable to eat. For example, request that regular marinara sauce be subbed for that Alfredo you're about to order. Also make sure to ask for extra veggies!

Side dishes are an easy place to slip up, but they're also an easy way to make huge improvements. Instead of ordering fries, upgrade to that salad. Drinks are also an easy place to go wrong: a glass of red wine or sparkling water is a great alternative to sugary soda and beer.

Don't be afraid to pack up your food for later. In fact, you should almost never finish a full meal at a restaurant. Restaurants are designed to leave people satisfied, no matter what their appetites are. Take me for a second. I'm not a very tall woman, but the restaurant will serve me the same size meal as my husband who is over six feet tall!

I recommend skipping dessert for the most part. Unless the restaurant has a fruit bowl, opt for tea or coffee instead. If skipping just isn't an option, make sure to split the dish with your partner.

Shopping Guide

Every ingredient in this book can be sourced at your local grocery store, but I definitely recommend exploring other shops as well. Find the best fishmonger. Check out your neighborhood butcher. Make sure to pick up seasonal fruits and veggies from your farmer's market. And source bread from your local bakery, if they serve whole wheat. Make sure to talk to these people; they're often highly knowledgeable about food and will make recommendations based on your diet and aspirations.

I highly recommend making ingredient substitutions based on what you can find locally! When shopping at the grocery store, stay away from prepackaged foods. Try to stick to the fresh-food aisles. The freezer section can also be handy for grabbing food that is currently out of season.

It may be difficult at first to figure out your shopping routine, but begin to take note of where the healthier-choice ingredients are kept, and you'll be in and out of the grocery store in no time.

Thank You

Before I let you dive into the recipes, I just want to thank you for picking up and reading this book. It means so much to me that you've decided to incorporate my recipes into your life.

Enjoy! And I can't wait to see you in the community.

-Erika Simons

Breakfast

RECIPES

Serves: 2

This rich and creamy fig smoothie is a great way to start your day, particularly if you need something quick and easy. This smoothie not only tastes delicious but will also assist with balancing energy levels, as it is full of both complex carbohydrates and good-quality healthy fats. Figs are also known as the fruit of the gods and are full of fiber, vitamins, minerals and antioxidants, all of which are going to help support your overall health and well-being.

Breakfast Fig Smoothie

INGREDIENTS

4 large fresh figs, cut into quarters

2 small/medium frozen bananas, sliced

¼ cup natural Greek yogurt

3 tbsp. oats

3 tbsp. almonds

2 tbsp. honey

1 tbsp. chia seeds

1 cup water

1 cup ice

INSTRUCTIONS

1. Combine all the ingredients in a high-speed blender and process on high for 1 minute or until smooth. Add more liquid if necessary to adjust thickness, and blend again.

2. Divide between two tall glasses and serve immediately.

NUTRITION DATA FOR 1 SERVING:

Calories **470kcal**	Sodium **41mg**
Total Carbohydrates **81g**	Potassium **915mg**
Protein **11g**	Dietary Fiber **12g**
Total Fat **15g**	Sugars **57g**
Saturated Fat **2g**	Vitamin A **6% Daily Value**
Polyunsaturated Fat **3g**	Vitamin C **19% Daily Value**
Monounsaturated Fat **7g**	Calcium **51% Daily Value**
Trans Fat **0g**	Iron **14% Daily Value**
Cholesterol **3mg**	

Caprese Breakfast Tart

Serves: 8

Do you have a few mouths to feed at breakfast time? Or perhaps you're hosting a special brunch? This Caprese Breakfast Tart is a wonderful option as a slice-and-share meal that everyone is going to love. The classic flavors of tomato, cheese and fresh basil work well together—so well, in fact, that there is no need to add to them or make the tart any more complicated—if it's not broken, don't fix it!

This simple yet impressive breakfast dish can be served either hot or cold ... either way, it will be gone before you know it.

INGREDIENTS

1 large sheet puff pastry

2 tbsp. olive oil

36 thin slices tomato

36 thin slices fresh buffalo-milk mozzarella

¼ cup freshly grated Parmesan cheese

¼ cup torn fresh basil leaves

INSTRUCTIONS

1. Preheat the oven to 425°F. Line a baking sheet with nonstick paper.

2. Lay the puff pastry sheet out flat on the lined baking sheet. Lightly brush the pastry with 1 tablespoon of the olive oil throughout.

3. Lay out three rows of 12 tomato slices and 12 mozzarella cheese slices on the pastry, alternating as you go and overlapping slightly, ensuring you leave a ½-inch to 1-inch border around all sides.

4. Once all three rows are arranged, drizzle over the remaining tablespoon of olive oil and sprinkle with the Parmesan cheese.

5. Bake 30–35 minutes or until golden.

6. Remove from the oven and sprinkle with the fresh basil leaves. Slice and serve immediately.

NUTRITION DATA FOR 1 SERVING:

Calories **377kcal**	Sodium **190mg**
Total Carbohydrates **17g**	Potassium **191mg**
Protein **19g**	Dietary Fiber **1g**
Total Fat **28g**	Sugars **2g**
Saturated Fat **9g**	Vitamin A **15% Daily Value**
Polyunsaturated Fat **7g**	Vitamin C **15% Daily Value**
Monounsaturated Fat **6g**	Calcium **24% Daily Value**
Trans Fat **0g**	Iron **6% Daily Value**
Cholesterol **40mg**	

Cottage Cheese Blueberry Casserole

Serves: 6

When serving this Cottage Cheese Blueberry Casserole for breakfast, you may think that you're having dessert instead. Don't be fooled. While it is absolutely delicious, this meal is also loaded with protein and low in sugar, which makes the recipe a great option to start the day. Next time you want to go to a little extra effort and create something special for your morning meal, give this dish a go. Though leftovers are unlikely, they can be served for a snack or even an after-dinner treat. Enjoy!

INGREDIENTS

4 eggs, separated

⅔ cup monk fruit sweetener (or natural sugar of choice)

⅔ cup flour, sifted

2 tbsp. freshly squeezed lemon juice

2 tsp. finely grated lemon peel

1 tsp. vanilla extract

1 tsp. almond extract

½ tsp. salt

2 cups cottage cheese

1 cup sour cream

1½ cups fresh blueberries

INSTRUCTIONS

1. Preheat the oven to 300°F and lightly grease an 8-inch casserole dish. Set aside.

2. In a medium bowl, beat the egg yolks until light. Blend in the sweetener, spelt flour, lemon juice, lemon peel, vanilla, almond extract, and salt.

3. Place the cottage cheese into a large bowl, then add a small amount of the egg yolk mixture and beat on high speed until the curds are broken and the mixture is nearly smooth.

4. Add the remaining egg yolk mixture and the sour cream. Beat until blended.

5. In a separate bowl, beat thde egg whites until stiff but not dry, then fold into the cheese mixture.

6. Pour into the greased casserole dish. Place in the oven and bake for 40 minutes.

7. Remove from the oven and sprinkle the blueberries on top in an even layer. Continue to bake for another 20 minutes. Refrigerate at least 5 hours before serving.

NUTRITION DATA FOR 1 SERVING:

Calories **244kcal**	Sodium **542mg**
Total Carbohydrates **41g**	Potassium **134mg**
Protein **18g**	Dietary Fiber **2g**
Total Fat **10g**	Sugars **29g**
Saturated Fat **6g**	Vitamin A **11% Daily Value**
Polyunsaturated Fat **1g**	Vitamin C **9% Daily Value**
Monounsaturated Fat **2g**	Calcium **11% Daily Value**
Trans Fat **0.6g**	Iron **8% Daily Value**
Cholesterol **165mg**	

Easy Breakfast Pizza

Serves: 4

This recipe for Easy Breakfast Pizza uses a simple dough that is quick and easy to make, and there's no need for a lengthy proofing time. Topped with plenty of your favorite breakfast ingredients, this is essentially a "Big Breakfast" or "Breakfast with the Works"—just made into a pizza (genius, right?).

Serve the pizza in the middle of the table and watch it quickly disappear. If you have a few mouths to feed, we suggest you double the batch to ensure you get a slice of your own to enjoy before it's all gobbled up.

INGREDIENTS

1½ cups self-rising flour, plus more for kneading

1 cup plain Greek yogurt

2 tbsp. olive oil

½ cup arugula leaves

⅓ cup sliced mushrooms

¼ cup cream cheese

5 slices prosciutto, chopped

3 eggs

⅓ cup freshly grated Parmesan cheese

salt and pepper, to taste

INSTRUCTIONS

1. Preheat the oven to 450°F. Lightly grease a 12-inch pizza pan.

2. In a mixing bowl, mix together the flour and the yogurt, using your hands if necessary.

3. Tip out onto a floured flat surface and knead together for approximately 10 minutes, adding more flour as necessary to prevent from sticking.

4. Place the dough on the prepared pan and, starting from the center, spread it to the edges of the pan.

5. Bake for 6 minutes, until the base just begins to brown, then remove from the oven.

6. Spread the olive oil over the crust, then sprinkle with the arugula and mushrooms.

7. Drop dollops of the cream cheese one teaspoon at a time over the top of the pizza, then arrange the prosciutto in an even fashion on the top.

8. Carefully crack the eggs on top of the pizza, toward the center so they do not run off the edge. Sprinkle with Parmesan cheese and a good crack of salt and pepper.

9. Bake for an additional 10 to 15 minutes or until the toppings are thoroughly heated, the eggs are cooked to your liking and the crust is a deep golden brown.

10. Slice and serve immediately.

NUTRITION DATA FOR 1 SERVING:

Calories **428kcal**	Sodium **1142mg**
Total Carbohydrates **40g**	Potassium **335mg**
Protein **19g**	Dietary Fiber **1g**
Total Fat **21g**	Sugars **5g**
Saturated Fat **8g**	Vitamin A **9% Daily Value**
Polyunsaturated Fat **2g**	Vitamin C **1% Daily Value**
Monounsaturated Fat **9g**	Calcium **39% Daily Value**
Trans Fat **2.3g**	Iron **17% Daily Value**
Cholesterol **174mg**	

Serves: 6

This is no ordinary fruit salad. The addition of Italian ricotta balances the flavors perfectly. The walnuts also add a little texture, while the cranberries give a subtle but divine tang. This impressive breakfast dish is surprisingly simple to make and can be tossed together in no more than 10 minutes (with time to spare). If you need to eat on the run, you can simply assemble your salad in a mason jar to make it the perfect portable breakfast.

Fruit Salad with Italian Ricotta

INGREDIENTS

2 large apples, cored and thinly sliced

2 large Nashi pears, cored and thinly sliced

1 cup fresh baby spinach leaves

⅓ cup dried cranberries

⅓ cup finely chopped walnuts

⅔ cup Italian ricotta

2½ tbsp. raw honey

½ tbsp. freshly squeezed lemon juice

½ tsp. ground cinnamon

INSTRUCTIONS

1. In a salad bowl, toss together the apples, pears, spinach, dried cranberries and walnuts.

2. In a separate bowl, whip together the Italian ricotta, honey, lemon juice and cinnamon. Add to the fruit mixture and toss to combine. Serve immediately.

NUTRITION DATA FOR 1 SERVING:

Calories **309kcal**	Sodium **125mg**
Total Carbohydrates **27g**	Potassium **295mg**
Protein **15g**	Dietary Fiber **3g**
Total Fat **17g**	Sugars **16g**
Saturated Fat **8g**	Vitamin A **17% Daily Value**
Polyunsaturated Fat **4g**	Vitamin C **10% Daily Value**
Monounsaturated Fat **4g**	Calcium **30% Daily Value**
Trans Fat **1.7g**	Iron **5% Daily Value**
Cholesterol **48mg**	

Golden Millet Porridge

Serves: 4

How awesome is it to start your day with a bowl of warm, comforting porridge? This recipe is a little different from what you may have grown up with. We have swapped the oats for millet and added a few Mediterranean-inspired ingredients. This Golden Millet Porridge is packed full of goodness, is nutrient dense and promotes many health benefits. Not only is it good for your health, it will also do wonders for your soul as it is the ultimate comfort breakfast meal.

INGREDIENTS

PORRIDGE:

1½ cups millet, uncooked

½ cup diced apple

½ cup diced butternut squash

3 cups milk of choice

2 cups water

½ tsp. ground cinnamon

¼ tsp. sea salt

TO SERVE:

2 tbsp. honey

¼ cup roughly chopped walnuts

¼ cup raisins

1 pinch ground cinnamon

INSTRUCTIONS

1. Combine all the porridge ingredients in a large saucepan and bring to a boil over low-medium heat.

2. Cover and reduce the heat, then allow to simmer until the liquid is absorbed, and the millet, squash and apple are tender, approximately 25 minutes.

3. To serve, divide the porridge among serving bowls. Drizzle with a little honey, a sprinkle of walnuts and raisins and a pinch of ground cinnamon. Feel free to also add a dash of milk if you wish.

NUTRITION DATA FOR 1 SERVING:

Calories **512kcal**
Total Carbohydrates **83g**
Protein **16g**
Total Fat **14g**
Saturated Fat **4g**
Polyunsaturated Fat **6g**
Monounsaturated Fat **3g**
Trans Fat **1.4g**
Cholesterol **18mg**
Sodium **226mg**
Potassium **539mg**
Dietary Fiber **8g**
Sugars **24g**
Vitamin A **32% Daily Value**
Vitamin C **8% Daily Value**
Calcium **24% Daily Value**
Iron **15% Daily Value**

Toast for breakfast is a big favorite for many families. However, it can quickly become a little boring, particularly if all you're doing is spreading on jam or honey every morning. Mix things up a little and create some excitement around breakfast by adding a gourmet touch to your simple sliced toast.

The flavor of the feta cheese goes perfectly with the tomato and avocado, while the squeeze of citrus and the sprinkle of pomegranate ariels bring flavors that pop and impress. Feel free to toast your preferred style of bread; however, sourdough does go beautifully.

Gourmet Feta Toast

INGREDIENTS

4 slices toast of choice (rye/ sourdough/ multigrain)

½ cup soft Greek feta cheese

2 small tomatoes, thinly sliced

1 avocado, thinly sliced

¼ cup pomegranate ariels

2 tbsp. pepitas

2 tbsp. flaxseed sprouts (optional)

4 lemon (or lime) wedges

INSTRUCTIONS

1. Prepare your toast according to your liking. Once done, transfer the slices to serving plates.
2. Spread each slice of toast with the feta cheese. Top with the slices of tomato and avocado, then sprinkle over the pomegranate ariels, pepitas and flaxseed sprouts, if using.
3. Serve immediately with a lemon or lime wedge to squeeze over the top.

NUTRITION DATA FOR 1 SERVING:

Calories **223kcal**	Sodium **318mg**
Total Carbohydrates **22g**	Potassium **372mg**
Protein **7g**	Dietary Fiber **5g**
Total Fat **12g**	Sugars **3g**
Saturated Fat **3g**	Vitamin A **12% Daily Value**
Polyunsaturated Fat **2g**	Vitamin C **26% Daily Value**
Monounsaturated Fat **6g**	Calcium **5% Daily Value**
Trans Fat **0.3g**	Iron **8% Daily Value**
Cholesterol **11mg**	

Lemon Ricotta Pancakes

Serves: 3 (about 6 large pancakes)

Many people have fond memories from childhood of sharing a plate of pancakes for breakfast on a special occasion. Next time you're whipping up a batch, whether it be for a birthday breakfast or a weekend treat, give these Lemon Ricotta Pancakes a try. We promise you will love them, and they just might become one of your new favorites.

These are best served warm with a slather of butter, a squeeze of lemon juice and a dusting of sugar. You may also want to cook up a double batch, as everyone will keep coming back for more.

INGREDIENTS

- ⅔ cup ricotta cheese
- 2 large eggs, separated
- ¼ cup milk of choice
- ¼ cup plus 2 tbsp. whole-wheat flour
- 2 tsp. sugar
- ¼ tsp. baking powder
- ⅛ tsp. salt
- 1 tbsp. finely minced lemon peel
- 1 tsp. finely minced lemon verbena
- 2 tsp. olive oil

INSTRUCTIONS

1. The night before, place the cheese in a piece of cheesecloth or a paper coffee filter and set in a strainer over a bowl. Cover with plastic wrap and refrigerate. In the morning, discard the whey collected in the bowl.
2. Transfer the drained ricotta to a food processor or blender, add the egg yolks, and process until smooth.
3. Add the milk, flour, sugar, baking powder and salt and process until completely blended.
4. Fold in the lemon peel and lemon verbena.
5. Beat the egg whites in a mixing bowl until just stiff but still moist, then fold gently into the batter.
6. Heat the olive oil in a large nonstick skillet over medium heat. Drop batter by 1⁄4 cupfuls onto the skillet and cook until the tops bubble. Turn and cook on the second side until golden brown.
7. Repeat with the remaining batter.
8. Serve immediately with your favorite toppings, such as lemon juice with a dusting of sugar or a drizzle of fresh local honey.

NUTRITION DATA FOR 1 SERVING:

Calories **135kcal**	Sodium **122mg**
Total Carbohydrates **11g**	Potassium **79mg**
Protein **6g**	Dietary Fiber **1g**
Total Fat **8g**	Sugars **3g**
Saturated Fat **3g**	Vitamin A **6% Daily Value**
Polyunsaturated Fat **0.5g**	Vitamin C **2% Daily Value**
Monounsaturated Fat **2g**	Calcium **10% Daily Value**
Trans Fat **2g**	Iron **4% Daily Value**
Cholesterol **89mg**	

Serves: 6

This is a fantastic recipe to prepare ahead of time and makes the ideal family breakfast. Warming, nourishing and full of Mediterranean-inspired flavors, it's perfect for breakfasts when the mornings begin to get a little cooler. You can make it the night before to have it ready for the next morning, or prepare it ahead of time and pop it in the freezer for the days or weeks to come. Just make sure it is well defrosted before baking.

Leftovers can also become a fantastic lunch or even dinner option, making this dish an all-around great family favorite.

Overnight Breakfast Strata

INGREDIENTS

12 slices sourdough bread, cubed

1 lb. ground pork

⅓ cup chopped onion

⅓ cup chopped green pepper

1 (4-oz.) jar pimientos, drained and chopped

6 large eggs

3 cups milk

½ cup cubed feta cheese

2 tsp. Worcestershire sauce

2 tsp. fresh oregano

1 tsp. ground mustard

½ tsp. sea salt

¼ tsp. pepper

INSTRUCTIONS

1. Lightly grease a 9-by-13-inch baking pan or casserole dish and spread in the bread cubes; set aside.
2. In a skillet over medium heat, combine the ground pork, onion and green pepper. Cook until the pork is browned, then drain off any excess fat.
3. Stir in the pimientos, then sprinkle the pork and vegetable mixture over the bread.
4. In a bowl, beat together the eggs, milk, feta cheese, Worcestershire sauce, oregano, mustard, salt and pepper and carefully pour over the pork mixture. Cover and refrigerate overnight.
5. The next day, remove the strata from the fridge and allow to come to room temperature.
6. Preheat the oven to 325°F.
7. Bake, covered, for 1 hour and 20 minutes.
8. Uncover and bake 10 minutes longer or until a knife inserted near the center comes out clean.
9. Let stand for 10 minutes before serving.

NUTRITION DATA FOR 1 SERVING:

Calories **426kcal**	Monounsaturated Fat **7g**	Sugars **6g**
Total Carbohydrates **42g**	Trans Fat **0.9g**	Vitamin A **11% Daily Value**
Protein **20g**	Cholesterol **57mg**	Vitamin C **33% Daily Value**
Total Fat **17g**	Sodium **695mg**	Calcium **16% Daily Value**
Saturated Fat **8g**	Potassium **349mg**	Iron **16% Daily Value**
Polyunsaturated Fat **1g**	Dietary Fiber **1g**	

Serves: 4

This rich and hearty Spanish-inspired breakfast dish is both extremely flavorful and nourishing. The dish offers warmth and depth and will quickly become a popular breakfast choice. If you are pressed for time in the mornings, it can be made a day or two ahead as it reheats well. In fact, we think it tastes even better when made like this, since it allows extra time for the rich flavors to develop. Serve on top of a slice of toast or alongside a crusty baguette. A sprinkle of shaved Parmesan and fresh parsley on top would go nicely too.

Spanish Breakfast Beans

INGREDIENTS

2 cups chicken or vegetable stock

1 small potato, diced

½ medium bell pepper, seeded and finely diced

1½ tsp. garlic powder

2 tbsp. sofrito

1 tsp. sazon, or a little more to taste

3 tbsp. tomato sauce

1 (14-oz.) can pinto beans

TO SERVE:

freshly squeezed lemon juice, to taste

salt and pepper, to taste

crusty bread or toast

INSTRUCTIONS

1. Combine all the ingredients in a medium saucepan over medium heat. Boil until the vegetables are tender and cooked through, approximately 20 minutes.
2. Season with a squeeze of lemon juice and salt and black pepper, to taste.
3. Serve over or alongside crusty bread or toast if desired.

NUTRITION DATA FOR 1 SERVING:

Calories **150kcal**	Sodium **697mg**
Total Carbohydrates **23g**	Potassium **306mg**
Protein **7g**	Dietary Fiber **6g**
Total Fat **2g**	Sugars **4g**
Saturated Fat **0.02g**	Vitamin A **15% Daily Value**
Polyunsaturated Fat **0.1g**	Vitamin C **66% Daily Value**
Monounsaturated Fat **0.005g**	Calcium **5% Daily Value**
Trans Fat **2g**	Iron **10% Daily Value**
Cholesterol **0mg**	

Stuffed Mushrooms

Serves: 4

These Stuffed Mushrooms are super easy to make, delicious to taste and a fantastic way to start the day. Crammed full of vegetables, this breakfast meal will ensure you are properly fueled to tackle anything coming your way that day.

These mushrooms are not only a great meal option, they are also a celebration of simple Mediterranean flavors that go perfectly together on a plate. If you want to take this recipe to another level, you can also serve with a little shaved Parmesan cheese, or even melt a little Parmesan cheese on top.

INGREDIENTS

8 large portobello mushrooms

6 tbsp. extra-virgin olive oil

1 onion, finely diced

1 clove garlic, minced

1 zucchini, finely diced

1 bell pepper, seeded and finely diced

2 tomatoes, finely diced

3 tbsp. chopped fresh chives

½ tbsp. freshly squeezed lemon juice

salt and pepper, to taste

INSTRUCTIONS

1. Preheat the oven to 350°F.
2. Wipe the mushrooms clean and remove their stems (save for another use).
3. Lightly cover a baking sheet with 2 tablespoons of the oil and lay on the mushrooms stem side up.
4. Pour ½ teaspoon of olive oil over each one and bake 20–30 minutes.
5. Meanwhile, heat the remaining 1 tablespoon of olive oil in a nonstick skillet over medium heat.
6. Add the onion and garlic and sauté for 5 minutes. Add the zucchini and bell pepper and continue to sauté 10–15 minutes until soft. Add the diced tomatoes and chives and cook for 5 minutes more, then season the vegetables with the lemon juice and salt and pepper, to taste.
7. Remove the mushrooms from the oven. Fill each mushroom cap with the vegetable mixture and serve.

NUTRITION DATA FOR 1 SERVING:

Calories **194kcal**
Total Carbohydrates **18g**
Protein **9g**
Total Fat **11g**
Saturated Fat **2g**
Polyunsaturated Fat **1g**
Monounsaturated Fat **8g**
Trans Fat **0g**
Cholesterol **0mg**
Sodium **33mg**
Potassium **318mg**
Dietary Fiber **9g**
Sugars **7g**
Vitamin A **28% Daily Value**
Vitamin C **107% Daily Value**
Calcium **2% Daily Value**
Iron **2% Daily Value**

Serves: 4

This Tortilla Española is a traditional Spanish omelet and is full of vibrant, rich Mediterranean flavors. We're not sure if the best part of this omelet is how delicious it tastes, how filling it is, or how super easy is to make—and all in one pan. This saves big time on washing up. But we guarantee you will love it just as much, perhaps even for an added reason of your own.

If you don't mind going to a little extra effort (or creating more dishes to wash), you could also transfer your Tortilla Española mixture to 4 individual ramekins before placing in the oven to cook. This is a great option if you'd like to serve individual portions for each person.

Tortilla Española

INGREDIENTS

2 tbsp. olive oil

2 small/medium potatoes, scrubbed and diced

1 Italian sausage, sliced (5 oz.)

1 onion, peeled and sliced thin

3 cloves garlic, minced

1 small/medium red bell pepper, seeded and sliced

6 eggs, beaten

salt and pepper, to taste

INSTRUCTIONS

1. Preheat the oven to 375°F.
2. In a large cast iron skillet or Dutch oven, heat the olive oil over medium heat.
3. Add the potatoes, sausage, onion, and garlic and sauté until the potatoes are soft, the onions are translucent and the sausage is cooked through.
4. Add the bell pepper and toss to combine.
5. In a bowl, beat the eggs well and season with salt and pepper.
6. Pour the eggs over the potatoes and sausages in the skillet and swirl around so the eggs coat the pan evenly.
7. Place the cast iron skillet in the oven and bake for approximately 20 minutes or until eggs are cooked through. When the center is set and the top is slightly brown, the tortilla is done.
8. Remove from the oven and allow to sit for 5 minutes. Run a knife around the outside of the skillet and invert onto a round platter. Serve at room temperature.

NUTRITION DATA FOR 1 SERVING:

Calories **455kcal**	Monounsaturated Fat **16g**	Sugars **3g**
Total Carbohydrates **20g**	Trans Fat **0.2g**	Vitamin A **25% Daily Value**
Protein **19g**	Cholesterol **52mg**	Vitamin C **93% Daily Value**
Total Fat **33g**	Sodium **1123mg**	Calcium **3% Daily Value**
Saturated Fat **10g**	Potassium **631mg**	Iron **10% Daily Value**
Polyunsaturated Fat **4g**	Dietary Fiber **3g**	

Lunch

RECIPES

Avgolemono Lemon Chicken Soup

Serves: 6

You will love this original Greek recipe for Avgolemono Lemon Chicken Soup. *Ahvo-lemon-o*, as the Greeks pronounce it, is a silky, rich and fragrant chicken soup, prepared Greek style with avgolemono sauce. This soup can be made in just under 30 minutes!

INGREDIENTS

1 tbsp. extra-virgin olive oil

½ to 1 cup carrots, finely chopped

½ to 1 cup celery, finely chopped

½ to 1 cup green onions, finely chopped

2 cloves garlic, finely chopped

8 cups low-sodium chicken broth

2 bay leaves

1 cup white rice

salt and black pepper, to taste

6–8 oz. boneless chicken breast, cooked and shredded (store-bought rotisserie chicken will work)

½ cup freshly squeezed lemon juice

2 large eggs

fresh parsley for garnish (optional)

INSTRUCTIONS

1. Over medium heat, heat the olive oil in a medium saucepan. Add the carrots, celery and green onions. Toss together to sauté briefly, then stir in the garlic.

2. Add the chicken broth and bay leaves, then raise the heat to high. When the liquid comes to a boil, immediately add the rice, salt and pepper. Adjust the heat to medium-low and simmer uncovered for 20 minutes or until the rice is tender. Stir in the cooked chicken.

3. To prepare the egg-lemon sauce, whisk together the lemon juice and eggs in a medium bowl. While whisking, add two ladlefuls of the broth from the cooking pot to help temper the eggs. Once fully combined, add the sauce to the chicken soup and stir. Remove from the heat immediately.

4. Garnish with fresh parsley if you like. Serve hot with your favorite bread and enjoy!

NUTRITION DATA FOR 1 SERVING:

Calories **266kcal**
Total Carbohydrates **33g**
Protein **17g**
Total Fat **7g**
Saturated Fat **2g**
Polyunsaturated Fat **3g**
Monounsaturated Fat **2g**
Trans Fat **0.1g**
Cholesterol **135mg**
Sodium **347mg**
Potassium **214mg**
Dietary Fiber **0.4g**
Sugars **2g**
Vitamin A **6% Daily Value**
Vitamin C **11% Daily Value**
Calcium **28% Daily Value**
Iron **9% Daily Value**

Serves: 4

This homemade Chicken Souvlaki with Tzatziki recipe takes you to the streets of Athens, complete with the best souvlaki marinade! The word *souvlaki* simply means "meat on skewers." But Greeks also use it to describe the actual meal—warm pita, loaded with perfectly marinated grilled meat and topped with tzatziki sauce. Even a handful of fries is sometimes tucked into the pita, though here we've chosen to use a healthier selection of fixings.

Chicken Souvlaki with Tzatziki

INGREDIENTS

FOR THE SOUVLAKI MARINADE:

10 cloves garlic, peeled

2 tbsp. dried oregano

1 tsp. dried rosemary

1 tsp. sweet paprika

1 tsp. each kosher salt and black pepper

¼ cup extra-virgin olive oil

¼ cup dry white wine

1 lemon, juiced

FOR THE CHICKEN:

2½ lb. organic boneless skinless chicken breast, fat removed, cut into 1½-inch pieces

2 bay leaves

INSTRUCTIONS

1. In the bowl of a food processor, combine the garlic, oregano, rosemary, paprika, salt, pepper, olive oil, white wine and lemon juice. Pulse until well combined.

2. Place the chicken in a large bowl and add the bay leaves. Top with the marinade. Toss to combine, making sure the chicken is well coated with the marinade. Cover tightly and refrigerate for at least 2 hours or overnight.

3. Soak 10 to 12 wooden skewers in water for 30-40 minutes. Meanwhile, prepare the tzatziki sauce and other fixings, and if you're adding Greek salad or other sides, prepare those as well.

4. Thread the marinated chicken pieces onto the prepared skewers. Reserve the marinade.

5. Brush the grates of an outdoor grill or a griddle with a little oil and heat to medium-high. Place the chicken skewers on the grill (or cook in batches on the griddle, if necessary). Cook, turning skewers to grill evenly on all sides and brushing lightly with the remaining marinade, until well browned and the internal temperature registers 155°F on an instant-read thermometer, about 5 minutes total.

PITA FIXINGS:

Smooth Tzatziki (page 200)

sliced tomato, cucumber, onions and kalamata olives

Greek pita bread

IDEAS TO SERVE ALONGSIDE (OPTIONAL):

Simple Greek Salad (page 68)

roasted garlic hummus

mezze platter

6. Discard any leftover marinade. Transfer the chicken to a serving platter and let rest for 3 minutes. Meanwhile, briefly grill the pitas and keep warm.

7. Assemble the pitas: First, spread tzatziki sauce on each pita. Remove the chicken pieces from the skewers. Add the chicken to each pita, then add the veggies and the olives.

8. If you want more items to add to your buffet, consider Greek salad, watermelon salad or roasted garlic hummus.

NUTRITION DATA FOR 1 SERVING:

Calories **168kcal**	Sodium **705mg**
Total Carbohydrates **2g**	Potassium **261mg**
Protein **22g**	Dietary Fiber **2g**
Total Fat **8g**	Sugars **1g**
Saturated Fat **2g**	Vitamin A **4% Daily Value**
Monounsaturated Fat **3g**	Vitamin C **8% Daily Value**
Polyunsaturated Fat **1g**	Calcium **33% Daily Value**
Trans Fat **1g**	Iron **12% Daily Value**
Cholesterol **69mg**	

Italian Oven-Roasted Vegetables

Serves: 6

Simple Italian Oven-Roasted Vegetables: the perfect combination, lightly seasoned and tossed in extra-virgin olive oil. They can be the perfect gluten-free garnish, ready in just minutes. They also make a great main vegetarian entrée when served on top of rice or even quinoa. And for vegans, just skip the Parmesan.

INGREDIENTS

12 oz. baby potatoes, scrubbed (halved or quartered if large)

12 oz. Campari tomatoes (or grape or cherry tomatoes)

2 zucchini or summer squash, cut into 1-inch pieces

8 oz. baby bella mushrooms, cleaned, ends trimmed

10–12 large garlic cloves, peeled

¼ cup extra-virgin olive oil

½ tbsp. dried oregano

1 tsp. dried thyme

salt and pepper

freshly grated Parmesan cheese for serving (optional)

crushed red pepper flakes (optional)

INSTRUCTIONS

1. Preheat your oven to 375°F. Lightly grease a baking sheet with olive oil.

2. Place the potatoes, tomatoes, zucchini, mushrooms and garlic in a large bowl. Drizzle generously with the olive oil. Add the oregano, thyme, salt and pepper. Toss and mix to combine.

3. Spread potatoes on the prepared pan. Roast in the oven for 10 minutes, then add all the remaining vegetables. Return to the oven to roast for another 20 minutes until the veggies are fork-tender.

4. Serve immediately with a sprinkle of freshly grated Parmesan cheese and crushed red pepper flakes, if desired.

NUTRITION DATA FOR 1 SERVING:

Calories **88kcal**	Sodium **354mg**
Total Carbohydrates **14g**	Potassium **107 mg**
Protein **3g**	Dietary Fiber **0.8g**
Total Fat **3g**	Sugars **0.4g**
Saturated Fat **0.3g**	Vitamin A **6% Daily Value**
Polyunsaturated Fat **0.2g**	Vitamin C **3% Daily Value**
Monounsaturated Fat **2g**	Calcium **36% Daily Value**
Trans Fat **1g**	Iron **14% Daily Value**
Cholesterol **0.0mg**	

Zesty Lemon Rice

Serves: 6

You will love this brilliant and delicious Greek Lemon Rice made with onion, garlic, fresh lemon juice and herbs! This easy accompaniment pairs very well with a number of Mediterranean favorites, such as souvlaki, shrimp, Greek baked cod and many others!

INGREDIENTS

2 cups long grain rice

3 tbsp. extra-virgin olive oil

1 medium yellow onion, chopped (just over 1 cup)

1 garlic clove, minced

½ cup orzo pasta

2 lemons, juiced

2 cups low-sodium broth (chicken or vegetable broth will work)

pinch of salt

zest of 1 lemon

large handful fresh parsley, chopped

1 tsp. dried dill weed

INSTRUCTIONS

1. Thoroughly wash the rice and soak for at least 15 minutes in plenty of cold water. You should be able to easily break a grain of rice by simply pressing it between your thumb and index finger. Drain well.

2. In a large saucepan that has a lid, heat the olive oil over medium heat until it is shimmering but not smoking. Add the onions and cook for 3 to 4 minutes until translucent. Add the garlic and orzo pasta. Toss for a short time, until the orzo has gained some color, then stir in the rice. Toss to coat.

3. Add the lemon juice and broth. Bring the liquid to a rolling boil, then reduce the heat to low. Cover and let cook for about 20 minutes or until the liquid is fully absorbed and the rice is tender but not sticky.

4. Remove the rice from the heat. For best results, leave it covered and do not disturb the rice for about 10 minutes. Uncover and stir in the lemon zest, parsley, salt and dill weed. If you desire, add a few slices of lemon on top for garnish. Enjoy!

NUTRITION DATA FOR 1 SERVING:

Calories **145kcal**	Sodium **53mg**
Total Carbohydrates **18g**	Potassium **130mg**
Protein **3g**	Dietary Fiber **0g**
Total Fat **7g**	Sugars **0.5g**
Saturated Fat **2g**	Vitamin A **5% Daily Value**
Polyunsaturated Fat **2g**	Vitamin C **7% Daily Value**
Monounsaturated Fat **4g**	Calcium **24% Daily Value**
Trans Fat **0.3g**	Iron **15% Daily Value**
Cholesterol **0mg**	

Mediterranean Bean Salad

Serves: 8

Once you try this Mediterranean-style three-bean salad, you won't go back! This bean salad is very bright and has lots of flavors: crispy vegetables, fresh herbs, capers and zesty garlic-Dijon vinaigrette. It's an excellent side dish accompanying any dinner: light chicken with lemon, beef kebabs, gyros or salmon burgers!

INGREDIENTS

1 (15-oz.) can kidney beans, drained and rinsed

1 (15-oz.) can cannellini beans, drained and rinsed

1 (15-oz.) can chickpeas, cooked

1 green bell pepper, cored and chopped

1 red bell pepper, cored and chopped

½ English cucumber, diced

1 cup chopped red onions

1½ tbsp. capers

1 cup chopped fresh parsley

10–15 fresh mint leaves, torn or gently chopped

10–15 fresh basil leaves, torn or gently chopped

FOR THE GARLIC-DIJON VINAIGRETTE:

¼ cup extra-virgin olive oil

2 tbsp. lemon juice

½ tbsp. Dijon mustard

1–2 cloves garlic, minced

1 tsp. sugar

salt and black pepper

INSTRUCTIONS

1. In a medium bowl, combine the beans, chickpeas, peppers, cucumber, onions, capers and fresh herbs. Mix using a wooden spoon until evenly combined.

2. In a small bowl, combine all the vinaigrette ingredients. Whisk vigorously to combine.

3. Add the vinaigrette and cucumber to the salad bowl. Toss to coat.

4. For the best results, cover and refrigerate for a bit before serving so that the beans soak up the vinaigrette flavors. Give the salad another quick toss before serving!

NUTRITION DATA FOR 1 SERVING:

Calories **211kcal**	Sodium **476mg**
Total Carbohydrates **28g**	Potassium **340mg**
Protein **10g**	Dietary Fiber **6g**
Total Fat **8g**	Sugars **4g**
Saturated Fat **1g**	Vitamin A **2% Daily Value**
Polyunsaturated Fat **4g**	Vitamin C **5% Daily Value**
Monounsaturated Fat **2g**	Calcium **6% Daily Value**
Trans Fat **1g**	Iron **15% Daily Value**
Cholesterol **0mg**	

Serves: 6

This simple Mediterranean salad of finely chopped vegetables with plenty of fresh parsley and bulgur wheat, all topped with lime juice and olive oil, will make your taste buds dance.

Bulgur & Lime Tabouli

INGREDIENTS

½ cup extra-fine bulgur wheat

4 Roma tomatoes, very finely chopped

1 English cucumber, very finely chopped

2 bunches parsley, part of the stems removed, washed and well dried, very finely chopped

12–15 fresh mint leaves, stems removed, washed and well dried, very finely chopped

4 green onions, white and green parts, very finely chopped

salt

3–4 tbsp. lime juice (or lemon juice, if you prefer)

3–4 tbsp. extra-virgin olive oil

pita bread to serve (optional)

romaine lettuce leaves to serve (optional)

INSTRUCTIONS

1. Wash the bulgur wheat and soak it in water 5–7 minutes. Drain very well, getting rid of all the excess water. Once drained, cook in boiling water 16-18 minutes or until tender. Set aside.

2. Place the tomatoes in a colander to drain excess juice.

3. Combine the chopped vegetables, herbs and green onions in a mixing bowl or dish. Add the bulgur and season with salt. Mix gently. Add the the lime juice and olive oil and mix again.

4. For the best results, cover the tabouli and refrigerate for 30 minutes. Transfer to a serving platter. If you like, serve the tabouli with a side of pita and romaine lettuce leaves, which act as wraps or "boats" for the tabouli.

NUTRITION DATA FOR 1 SERVING:

Calories **190kcal**	Sodium **79mg**
Total Carbohydrates **25g**	Potassium **105mg**
Protein **3g**	Dietary Fiber **3g**
Total Fat **10g**	Sugars **8g**
Saturated Fat **3g**	Vitamin A **2% Daily Value**
Polyunsaturated Fat **2g**	Vitamin C **6% Daily Value**
Monounsaturated Fat **3g**	Calcium **13% Daily Value**
Trans Fat **2g**	Iron **9% Daily Value**
Cholesterol **13mg**	

Serves: 6

A light, fresh watermelon salad with cucumbers, creamy feta cheese, many fresh herbs and a bright honey-lime dressing!

Serve it along with other favorite summer dishes, like grilled chicken skewers, kofta, grilled shrimp, salmon, grilled zucchini salad, guacamole and more! It's easily the perfect dish for your next neighborhood party!

Watermelon & Mint Salad

INGREDIENTS

FOR THE HONEY VINAIGRETTE:

2 tbsp. honey

2 tbsp. lime juice

1-2 tbsp. extra-virgin olive oil

pinch of salt

FOR THE WATERMELON SALAD:

½ watermelon, peeled, cut into cubes

1 English cucumber, cubed (about 2 cups)

15 fresh mint leaves, chopped

15 fresh basil leaves, chopped

½ cup crumbled feta cheese, or more to taste

INSTRUCTIONS

1. Whisk together the honey, lime juice, olive oil and salt in a small bowl. Set aside.

2. In a large bowl, combine the watermelon, cucumbers, and fresh herbs.

3. Top the watermelon salad with the honey vinaigrette and gently toss to combine evenly. Top with the feta cheese and serve!

NUTRITION DATA FOR 1 SERVING:

Calories **192kcal**
Total Carbohydrates **36g**
Protein **4g**
Total Fat **6g**
Saturated Fat **2g**
Polyunsaturated Fat **1g**
Monounsaturated Fat **0.2g**
Trans Fat **2g**
Cholesterol **3mg**
Sodium **119mg**
Potassium **126mg**
Dietary Fiber **2g**
Sugars **30g**
Vitamin A **4% Daily Value**
Vitamin C **8% Daily Value**
Calcium **16% Daily Value**
Iron **11% Daily Value**

Traditional Olives & Feta Salad

Serves: 5

Greek salad (horiatiki) is an iconic Mediterranean recipe that is simply topped with a splash of Greek extra-virgin olive oil and a little red wine vinegar (or lemon juice).

This recipe is a truly traditional Greek salad with ripe tomatoes, cucumbers, bell peppers, onions and creamy feta cheese.

INGREDIENTS

4 medium juicy tomatoes, preferably organic

⅓ English cucumber, partially peeled in a striped pattern

1 green bell pepper, cored

1 medium red onion

½ cup pitted Greek kalamata olives

pinch salt

¼ cup extra-virgin olive oil

1–2 tbsp. red wine vinegar

½ cup (4 oz.) Greek feta cheese (do not crumble), or more to taste

½ tbsp. dried oregano

INSTRUCTIONS

1. Slice the tomatoes into wedges or large chunks. Cut the cucumber in half lengthwise, then slice into thick half-moons. Thinly slice the bell pepper into rings.

2. Cut the red onion in half and thinly slice into half-moons.

3. Combine the tomatoes, cucumber, pepper and onion in a large salad dish. Add a good handful of the kalamata olives.

4. Season with the salt, then pour the olive oil and vinegar over the salad.

5. Give everything a very gentle toss to mix. Do not overmix; this salad is not meant to be handled too much.

6. Finally, add the the feta blocks and sprinkle the dried oregano on top. Serve with crusty bread if desired.

NUTRITION DATA FOR 1 SERVING:

Calories **169kcal**	Sodium **137mg**
Total Carbohydrates **8g**	Potassium **102mg**
Protein **6g**	Dietary Fiber **24g**
Total Fat **14g**	Sugars **47g**
Saturated Fat **4g**	Vitamin A **3% Daily Value**
Polyunsaturated Fat **6g**	Vitamin C **8% Daily Value**
Monounsaturated Fat **3g**	Calcium **12% Daily Value**
Trans Fat **0g**	Iron **15% Daily Value**
Cholesterol **25mg**	

Serves: 6

This 20-minute meal contains 24 grams of protein and has only 261 calories per serving. To ensure the velvety texture of this cozy soup, whisk some of the hot broth into the eggs before adding them to the pot; this cooks them gently and prevents any curdling.

Lemon Chicken Soup

INGREDIENTS

1 tbsp. extra-virgin olive oil

⅓ cup cubed carrots

½ cup chopped yellow onion

2 tsp. minced fresh garlic

⅓ tsp. crushed red pepper

6 cups unsalted chicken stock

½ cup whole-wheat orzo

3 large eggs

¼ cup fresh lemon juice

3 cups shredded rotisserie chicken

3 cups chopped baby spinach

1¼ tsp. kosher salt

½ tsp. black pepper

3 tbsp. chopped fresh dill

INSTRUCTIONS

1. Heat the oil in a Dutch oven over medium-high heat. Add the carrot and onion and cook, stirring often, until both vegetables are softened, 3–4 minutes. Add the garlic and crushed red pepper and cook, stirring constantly, until fragrant, about 1 minute.

2. Add the stock to the Dutch oven, increase the heat to high, and bring to a boil. Add the orzo and cook, uncovered, until orzo is al dente, about 6 minutes.

3. Meanwhile, in a medium bowl whisk the eggs and lemon juice together until frothy. Once the orzo is done, carefully remove 1 cup boiling stock from the Dutch oven. Gradually add the hot stock to the egg–lemon juice mixture, whisking constantly to temper the eggs for about 1 minute. Pour the egg mixture back into the Dutch oven and stir to combine.

4. Lower the heat to medium-low and stir in the chicken, spinach, salt and pepper. Cook, stirring constantly, until the spinach wilts, about 1 minute. Divide the soup among 6 bowls; sprinkle each serving evenly with dill.

NUTRITION DATA FOR 1 SERVING:

Calories **261kcal**	Monounsaturated Fat **1g**	Sugars **3g**
Total Carbohydrates **16g**	Trans Fat **0.5g**	Vitamin A **11% Daily Value**
Protein **24g**	Cholesterol **34mg**	Vitamin C **7% Daily Value**
Total Fat **8g**	Sodium **641mg**	Calcium **24% Daily Value**
Saturated Fat **2g**	Potassium **435mg**	Iron **17% Daily Value**
Polyunsaturated Fat **4g**	Dietary Fiber **3g**	

Roasted Kale & Chickpea Salad

Serves: 4

This satisfying vegetable bowl is packed with crunch and color, thanks to the addition of crispy carrots and chickpeas, fresh kale and a shimmering avocado topping. It also offers your daily dose of fiber, which is key to losing weight and maintaining energy and healthy digestion.

Bulgur, also called broken wheat, is a quick-cooking whole grain. And these bowls make great lunches too!

INGREDIENTS

3 cups boiling water

½ cup bulgur

2 (15-oz.) cans unsalted chickpeas, rinsed and drained

1½ tbsp. canola oil

2 cups finely chopped carrots

4 cups chopped lacinato kale

½ cup sliced shallots

½ cup fresh flat-leaf parsley leaves

½ tsp. kosher salt, divided

½ tsp. black pepper

½ avocado, peeled and pitted

2 tbsp. extra virgin olive oil

1 tbsp. fresh lemon juice

1 tbsp. tahini (sesame seed paste), well stirred

1 clove garlic

¼ tsp. ground turmeric

INSTRUCTIONS

1. Combine the water and bulgur and cook 14-18 minutes or until tender, drain well and set aside to cool.

2. Pat the chickpeas dry with paper towels. Heat the canola oil in a large skillet over high heat. Add the chickpeas and carrots and cook, stirring occasionally, until chickpeas are browned, about 6 minutes. Add the kale, cover, and cook until the kale is slightly wilted and carrots are tender, about 2 minutes. Add the chickpea mixture, shallots, parsley, ¼ teaspoon of the salt, and the pepper to the bulgur; toss to combine.

3. In a food processor, process the avocado, olive oil, lemon juice, tahini, garlic, turmeric and remaining ¼ teaspoon salt until smooth. Divide the bulgur mixture among 4 bowls and drizzle each serving evenly with the avocado mixture.

NUTRITION DATA FOR 1 SERVING:

Calories **520kcal**
Total Carbohydrates **68g**
Protein **18g**
Total Fat **20g**
Saturated Fat **2g**
Polyunsaturated Fat **13g**
Monounsaturated Fat **4g**
Trans Fat **1g**
Cholesterol **62.7mg**
Sodium **495mg**
Potassium **364mg**
Dietary Fiber **16g**
Sugars **7g**
Vitamin A **6% Daily Value**
Vitamin C **13% Daily Value**
Calcium **28% Daily Value**
Iron **10% Daily Value**

Carpaccio

Serves: 4

Recipes don't get much easier than this. In fact, it is hardly even a recipe—more of an arrangement. The trick with this recipe is to place the beef filet in the freezer until it becomes a little firm and can be sliced paper-thin. The slices of beef with the zesty sauce, arugula and shaved Parmesan served on top of either fresh bread or toasted baguette are the perfect meal to serve up as a shared plate in the warmer months when you're trying to escape the heat.

INGREDIENTS

1 lb. beef filet

½ cup lemon juice

¼ cup red wine (or red wine vinegar, for a nonalcoholic option)

2 tbsp. chopped parsley

2 tbsp. capers, drained

1 small clove garlic, minced

1 tbsp. minced shallots

1 tbsp. prepared mustard

½ cup olive oil

salt, to taste

¼ cup arugula leaves

2 tbsp. freshly shaved Parmesan cheese

INSTRUCTIONS

1. Trim all the fat from the beef, then wrap the filet in foil and place in the freezer for 30 minutes to facilitate slicing.

2. While the meat is in freezer, make the sauce by combining the lemon juice, wine, parsley, capers, garlic, shallots and mustard in a medium bowl. Gradually pour in the olive oil in a steady stream, whisking constantly, then season with salt and refrigerate for at least 20 minutes.

3. Remove the meat from the freezer. With a very sharp, thin knife, slice meat on a diagonal into paper-thin slices.

4. Place the beef slices on a platter or individual plates. Drizzle over a little of the sauce.

5. Sprinkle the arugula leaves and Parmesan cheese over the filet slices.

6. Serve with either fresh or toasted sliced baguette, and with any additional sauce on the side.

NUTRITION DATA FOR 1 SERVING:

Calories **513kcal**	Sodium **303mg**
Total Carbohydrates **4g**	Potassium **506mg**
Protein **26g**	Dietary Fiber **0.4g**
Total Fat **43g**	Sugars **1g**
Saturated Fat **9g**	Vitamin A **4% Daily Value**
Polyunsaturated Fat **4g**	Vitamin C **28% Daily Value**
Monounsaturated Fat **27g**	Calcium **7% Daily Value**
Trans Fat **0.4g**	Iron **19% Daily Value**
Cholesterol **75mg**	

Serves: 6

To this day, I still think a nice and Simple Greek Salad is the best late-night or mid-afternoon snack. Light, fresh and crisp, it's just the perfect thing to hold you over until that next meal!

Simple Greek Salad

INGREDIENTS

4 cups mixed salad greens (spinach, arugula, kale, watercress, romaine, etc.)

3 medium tomatoes, diced (or 1½ cups halved cherry tomatoes)

1 large cucumber, sliced

1 cup feta cheese, crumbled

4 scallions, sliced

12 ripe black olives, pitted

1 tbsp. balsamic vinegar

⅓ cup Italian Dressing

INSTRUCTIONS

1. Combine the greens, tomatoes, cucumber, feta cheese, scallions, olives, and vinegar in a large serving bowl.
2. Drizzle with the dressing and lightly toss together.
3. Let stand for up to 15 minutes before serving to allow the flavors to combine.

NUTRITION DATA FOR 1 SERVING:

Calories **128kcal**	Sodium **458mg**
Total Carbohydrates **8g**	Potassium **313mg**
Protein **5g**	Dietary Fiber **2g**
Total Fat **9g**	Sugars **5g**
Saturated Fat **4g**	Vitamin A **120% Daily Value**
Polyunsaturated Fat **2g**	Vitamin C **19% Daily Value**
Monounsaturated Fat **3g**	Calcium **16% Daily Value**
Trans Fat **4g**	Iron **5% Daily Value**
Cholesterol **22mg**	

This quick, easy, and silky smooth Italian Dressing just hits that perfect spot for all those salads, vegetables and even bread! High in good Polyunsaturated fats, this will be sure to impress!

Italian Dressing

INGREDIENTS

½ cup olive oil

2 tbsp. freshly squeezed lemon juice

1 tbsp. white wine vinegar

¼ cup capers, drained

1 clove garlic, minced

1 scallion, minced

1 small dried red chili, sliced

½ tsp. pepper

½ tsp. fennel seed, crushed

INSTRUCTIONS

1. Combine all the ingredients in a jar with a tight-fitting lid and shake well.
2. Store with the lid tightly secured in the refrigerator for up to 7 days.

NUTRITION DATA FOR 1 SERVING:

Calories **164kcal**	Sodium **10mg**
Total Carbohydrates **1g**	Potassium **32mg**
Protein **0g**	Dietary Fiber **0g**
Total Fat **18g**	Sugars **0g**
Saturated Fat **2g**	Vitamin A **3% Daily Value**
Polyunsaturated Fat **2g**	Vitamin C **16% Daily Value**
Monounsaturated Fat **13g**	Calcium **1% Daily Value**
Trans Fat **0g**	Iron **1% Daily Value**
Cholesterol **0mg**	

Pickled Herring with Beet Dip Crostini

Serves: 6

These crostini look incredible and taste just as good. They are the perfect combination of flavors, colors and textures. Light, bright and uplifting, the dish offers a great mix of earthy, sweet and sour flavors, each mouthful offering a taste sensation. If you're after a super quick lunch option, we suggest you make the dip ahead of time. Store it in a tightly covered glass jar in the refrigerator for up to one week. Any leftover dip can be used as a snack with vegetable sticks or slices of toasted pita bread.

INGREDIENTS

FOR THE DIP:

1 lb. beets, cooked until soft, then peeled, and cut into chunks

4 oz. labneh

2 tbsp. minced shallots

1 tbsp. apple cider vinegar

½ tsp. ground mustard

½ tsp. dried thyme

½ tsp. dried tarragon

TO SERVE:

8 slices French baguette, toasted

1 tbsp. olive oil

12 oz. pickled herring, drained

½ Spanish onion, peeled and thinly sliced

½ gherkins, thinly sliced

2 tbsp. freshly squeezed lemon juice

INSTRUCTIONS

1. Brush the bread slices with a little olive oil on each side.
2. Place the bread either on a hot grill plate or under a hot broiler and grill on both sides until lightly brown. Remove from the heat and set aside.
3. Meanwhile, combine all the dip ingredients in a food processor or blender and process until smooth.
4. Adjust the seasonings, adding more vinegar to taste.
5. Slather each toast slice with the dip and top with 2 to 3 slices of the pickled herring, slices of the Spanish onion and gherkin, and a squeeze of lemon juice over the top.
6. Serve immediately.
7. Refrigerate any remaining dip in a tightly sealed container for up to 7 days.

NUTRITION DATA FOR 1 SERVING:

Calories **277kcal**
Total Carbohydrates **27g**
Protein **10g**
Total Fat **15g**
Saturated Fat **4g**
Polyunsaturated Fat **1g**
Monounsaturated Fat **6g**
Trans Fat **0g**
Cholesterol **18mg**
Sodium **669mg**
Potassium **247mg**
Dietary Fiber **3g**
Sugars **11g**
Vitamin A **11% Daily Value**
Vitamin C **10% Daily Value**
Calcium **7% Daily Value**
Iron **8% Daily Value**

Pita Breads with Roasted Lamb & Vegetables

Serves: 12

Have you got a crowd to feed? If so, then we have the perfect recipe for you!

Make the succulent lamb ahead of time as it takes a bit to prepare and then cook. Although it takes a while getting the lamb ready for serving, it is well worth the wait. At the time of serving, the pita breads will come together in no time at all. This lunch is also a fun dish for kids (or anyone, for that matter) to make their own, stuffing their pita breads with the lamb and filling ingredients as they like.

INGREDIENTS

FOR THE LAMB:

3½ lb. lamb shoulder, on the bone

2 tbsp. lemon juice

1 small clove garlic, peeled and crushed

1 tsp. crushed red pepper

1 tsp. ground coriander

1 tsp. ground ginger

½ tsp. freshly ground black pepper

FOR THE FILLING:

6 oz. pitted black olives, drained

2 medium tomatoes, diced

1 large red bell pepper, seeded and sliced

1 large zucchini, grated

1 red onion, peeled and thinly sliced

1 cup arugula leaves

¼ cup chopped Italian parsley leaves

2 tbsp. lemon juice

1 tbsp. balsamic vinegar

1 tbsp. olive oil

salt and pepper, to taste

TO SERVE:

6 white pita breads

INSTRUCTIONS

1. Prepare the lamb the day before.
2. Combine the lemon juice, garlic, crushed red pepper, coriander, ginger and black pepper. Rub this marinade all over the lamb, place in a roasting pan, cover with plastic wrap and chill in the fridge overnight.
3. The next day, preheat the oven to 400°F. Remove the lamb from the fridge 30 minutes before cooking to bring to room temperature.
4. Roast the lamb in the oven for 1 hour 20 minutes for rare, or up to 30 minutes longer if you prefer it well-done.
5. When the lamb is cooked, remove it from the oven, cover with foil and let it rest for about 30 minutes in the pan.
6. Meanwhile, combine all the filling ingredients in a serving bowl and gently toss together.
7. Using a very sharp knife, cut the lamb down either side of the bone, and trim and discard all the fat and any sinew. Dice the lamb into 1-inch cubes.
8. Spoon some of the lamb and vegetable filling into each pita bread, season with a little more salt and pepper if you wish, and serve.

NUTRITION DATA FOR 1 SERVING:

Calories **526kcal**
Total Carbohydrates **29g**
Protein **35g**
Total Fat **30g**
Saturated Fat **12g**
Polyunsaturated Fat **3g**
Monounsaturated Fat **13g**
Trans Fat **0.5g**
Cholesterol **122mg**
Sodium **660mg**
Potassium **538mg**
Dietary Fiber **2g**
Sugar **2g**
Vitamin A **25% Daily Value**
Vitamin C **63% Daily Value**
Calcium **9% Daily Value**
Iron **25% Daily Value**

Serves: 4

When wild salmon comes into season, be sure to put this recipe on the menu. Salmon is somewhat of a firm-fleshed fish, which means cooking a fillet under the broiler won't dry out the fish like it would other species.

The rich, strong flavor of the salmon balances wonderfully with the freshness of the herbs in the couscous along with the sweetness from the bell peppers. For a grain- and gluten-free alternative, you can swap the couscous for cooked quinoa.

Grilled Salmon on Herbed Couscous

INGREDIENTS

FOR THE GRILLED SALMON:

4 (6-oz.) salmon fillets (about 1½ lb.)

2 tbsp. olive oil

1 tsp. salt

1 tsp. black pepper

1 large zucchini, thinly sliced

FOR THE HERBED COUSCOUS:

1½ cups vegetable stock

1 tsp. olive oil

1 tbsp. chopped fresh thyme leaves

1 tbsp. chopped fresh parsley

INSTRUCTIONS

1. For the couscous, combine the stock, oil, thyme, parsley, pepper and bay leaf in a small saucepan and bring to a boil.

2. Add the couscous and mix well, then remove from the heat. Cover tightly and allow to stand for at least 5 minutes, or until all of the liquid has been absorbed. Mix in the bell pepper and tomatoes and set aside.

3. Meanwhile, preheat the broiler to high.

4. Rub the surface of the fish with 1 tablespoon of the olive oil and sprinkle with the salt and pepper.

5. Broil 3–4 minutes per side or until the fish is cooked through and just flakes with a fork (do not overcook or the fish will become tough).

6. While the fish is cooking, heat the remaining tablespoon of olive oil in a skillet over medium-high heat. Add the zucchini and cook until just tender and slightly golden, 5–8 minutes.

¼ tsp. freshly ground black pepper

1 bay leaf

1 cup couscous

½ cup yellow bell pepper, finely diced

½ cup tomatoes, finely diced

7. To serve, place a rounded ½ cup of couscous on each of 4 plates. Divide the zucchini among each plate, set a piece of the finished grilled fish over top.

8. Serve with a slice or two of fresh lemon or lime, if desired.

NUTRITION DATA FOR 1 SERVING:

Calories **441kcal**	Sodium **748mg**
Total Carbohydrates **39g**	Potassium **423mg**
Protein **38g**	Dietary Fiber **4g**
Total Fat **14g**	Sugars **4g**
Saturated Fat **3g**	Vitamin A **48% Daily Value**
Polyunsaturated Fat **1g**	Vitamin C **27% Daily Value**
Monounsaturated Fat **6g**	Calcium **9% Daily Value**
Trans Fat **0.5g**	Iron **16% Daily Value**
Cholesterol **113mg**	

Shrimp & Asparagus Salad

Serves: 4

Asparagus and shrimp are a match made in heaven. This salad is incredibly delicious, and, when drizzled with the creamy horseradish dressing, it is the ideal dish to be serving up in springtime when asparagus is super fresh and plentiful. With just a few simple ingredients, this salad is easy to make and can be whipped up in less than 10 minutes. It is best served immediately while warm and will go perfectly with a glass of white wine, such as a Pinot Grigio.

INGREDIENTS

FOR THE SALAD:

1 tbsp. olive oil

1 medium onion, peeled and diced

2 cloves garlic, minced

1 lb. asparagus, trimmed and cut into 1½-inch pieces

1 lb. shrimp, cooked, shelled and deveined

2 large tomatoes, cut into wedges

FOR THE DRESSING:

1 cup mayonnaise

¼ cup freshly squeezed lemon juice

¼ cup finely chopped parsley

1 tbsp. prepared horseradish

½ tsp. sea salt

½ tsp. freshly ground black pepper

½ tsp. celery seed

TO SERVE:

4 lemon wedges

INSTRUCTIONS

1. Heat the olive oil in a skillet over medium-high heat. Add the onion and garlic and sauté 3–5 minutes, or until tender.

2. Add the asparagus and shrimp and continue to sauté, tossing frequently, until the asparagus is barely tender and the shrimp is heated through, approximately 2 minutes. Remove from the heat and place in a serving bowl, then add the tomatoes and toss to combine.

3. In another small bowl, mix together the mayonnaise, lemon juice, parsley, horseradish, salt, pepper and celery seed.

4. Stir the dressing into the shrimp and asparagus salad.

5. Divide among serving bowls and serve each with a slice of lemon.

NUTRITION DATA FOR 1 SERVING:

Calories **467kcal**	Sodium **444mg**
Total Carbohydrates **26g**	Potassium **680mg**
Protein **35g**	Dietary Fiber **3g**
Total Fat **26g**	Sugars **8g**
Saturated Fat **4g**	Vitamin A **35% Daily Value**
Polyunsaturated Fat **12g**	Vitamin C **50% Daily Value**
Monounsaturated Fat **8g**	Calcium **2% Daily Value**
Trans Fat **0.1g**	Iron **40% Daily Value**
Cholesterol **242mg**	

Sicilian Eggplant Caponata

Serves: 8

Caponata is a traditional and popular eggplant dish that is delicious served with freshly baked crusty bread. It is often prepared as an appetizer; however, we love our Sicilian Eggplant Caponata as a lunch option. Place a serving dish of this Mediterranean goodness on the table along with slices of crusty baguette (or your bread of choice), and let everyone dig in. A lovely and easy vegetarian meal that is full of flavor and textures, this is a wonderful dish to share with friends.

INGREDIENTS

- 2 tbsp. olive oil, plus more as needed
- 1 large eggplant, cut into 1-inch cubes
- salt and pepper, to taste
- 2 medium onions, peeled and diced
- 3 celery stalks, sliced
- 1 lb. canned Italian plum tomatoes
- 10 green olives, pitted and quartered
- 2 cloves garlic, crushed
- ¼ cup white wine vinegar
- 2 tbsp. sugar
- ½ cup pine nuts
- ¼ cup capers

INSTRUCTIONS

1. Heat the olive oil in a large nonstick skillet over medium-high heat. Season the eggplant with salt and pepper. Add to the skillet and cook until tender, about 4-6 minutes. Remove from the pan and set aside.
2. Add the onion to the skillet, increasing a little more olive oil if necessary, and sauté until tender. Add the celery, tomatoes, olives and garlic. Reduce the heat to medium-low and cook for 10 minutes more.
3. Meanwhile, heat the vinegar in a small saucepan over medium heat. Stir in the sugar until it is dissolved.
4. Return the cooked eggplant to the skillet and add the pine nuts and capers.
5. Add the vinegar mixture to the skillet and mix thoroughly.
6. Season with salt and pepper, to taste, and cook for 5 minutes longer.
7. Serve chilled on top of a sliced baguette, grilled crostini or fresh slices of your preferred Italian-style bread.

NUTRITION DATA FOR 1 SERVING:

Calories **158kcal**	Sodium **441mg**
Total Carbohydrates **13g**	Potassium **375mg**
Protein **3g**	Dietary Fiber **4g**
Total Fat **11g**	Sugars **7g**
Saturated Fat **1g**	Vitamin A **8% Daily Value**
Polyunsaturated Fat **3g**	Vitamin C **16% Daily Value**
Monounsaturated Fat **6g**	Calcium **3% Daily Value**
Trans Fat **0g**	Iron **7% Daily Value**
Cholesterol **0mg**	

Spinach Torta

Serves: 6

Looking for an exciting way to get more greens into your diet? Well, this is it. This Spinach Torta is an easy and extremely tasty way to make sure you're getting your daily dose. Not only does it taste fantastic, it also looks incredibly inviting, which hopefully means those fussy eaters won't turn their noses up at the first sign of "green." Each mouthful is both bursting with flavor and boasts plenty of nutrients as well.

INGREDIENTS

1 (10-oz.) pie crust, premade or frozen

1 tbsp. Dijon mustard

FILLING:

4 tbasp. butter

9 oz. frozen spinach, thawed and well drained

½ cup red onion, peeled and diced

¼ cup chopped, dry (not oil-packed) sun-dried tomatoes

1 tsp. dried Italian seasoning

½ tsp. dried oregano leaves

¼ tsp. garlic powder

¼ tsp. salt

4 eggs, beaten

2 cups shredded mozzarella cheese

INSTRUCTIONS

1. Preheat the oven to 450°F.

2. Thaw the pie crust according to the package directions. Prepare a 10-inch slightly greased springform pan.

3. Place the crust in the pan, pressing into the bottom and up the sides. Spread the mustard over the bottom of the crust and bake 9–11 minutes or until the crust is lightly browned. Cool on a wire rack.

4. Reduce the oven temperature to 350°F.

5. Melt the butter in a large skillet over medium-low heat.

6. Add the spinach, onion and sun-dried tomatoes. Cook and stir for 5 to 7 minutes or until the onion is crisp-tender. Remove from the heat, then add the Italian seasoning, oregano, garlic powder and salt. Mix well.

7. In a large bowl, combine the eggs and cheese. Mix well. Stir in the spinach mixture until well combined.

8. Spoon evenly into the partially baked crust, and bake for 25 to 35 minutes or until golden brown on top.

9. Allow to stand for 10 minutes before removing from the pan and slicing.

NUTRITION DATA FOR 1 SERVING:

Calories **499kcal**
Total Carbohydrates **29g**
Protein **19g**
Total Fat **35g**
Saturated Fat **14g**
Polyunsaturated Fat **5g**
Monounsaturated Fat **12g**
Trans Fat **2.2g**
Cholesterol **181mg**
Sodium **810mg**
Potassium **317mg**
Dietary Fiber **4g**
Sugars **3g**
Vitamin A **114% Daily Value**
Vitamin C **20% Daily Value**
Calcium **38% Daily Value**
Iron **19% Daily Value**

Serves: 4

Eggplant is an extremely versatile vegetable and is the hero of so many Mediterranean dishes, just like this one. While there are many stuffed-eggplant recipes (and why not—who doesn't like a stuffed eggplant?), we love what we have created with this one. Using tuna and anchovies boosts this dish's nutritional profile and its flavor, which is then balanced out beautifully with the feta cheese, capers and olives. If you are after a vegetarian option, replace the anchovies and tuna with cooked chickpeas or cannellini beans that have been roughly chopped.

Tuna-Stuffed Eggplants

INGREDIENTS

2 large eggplants

1–2 tsp. coarsely ground sea salt

¼ cup olive oil

2 tomatoes, diced

1½ cups fresh bread crumbs

7 oz. canned tuna in water, drained

6 anchovy fillets, finely chopped

½ cup finely minced black olives

2 tbsp. minced capers

1 tbsp. finely chopped basil

1 tbsp. chopped Italian parsley

½ cup grated mozzarella cheese

½ cup crumbled feta cheese

INSTRUCTIONS

1. Preheat the oven to 375°F.

2. Cut the eggplants in half lengthwise and scoop out the flesh, leaving a ½" shell. Finely dice the pulp, sprinkle well with salt and place in a colander set in the sink.

3. Sprinkle the insides of the eggplant shells with salt and place them cut side down on a paper towel. Allow the eggplant pulp and shells to drain for 30 minutes.

4. Heat the olive oil in a large skillet over high heat. Add the well-drained eggplant pulp and cook until lightly browned. Add the tomatoes and stir until the liquid is evaporated, about 12 minutes.

5. Add the bread crumbs, tuna, anchovies, olives, capers, basil and parsley. Cook the mixture for 2 more minutes.

6. Place the eggplant shells in a foil-lined baking dish. Divide the eggplant-tomato mixture among the shells and sprinkle over the grated mozzarella cheese and crumbled feta cheese. Place in the oven and bake for 1 hour. Serve hot and crispy!

NUTRITION DATA FOR 1 SERVING:

Calories **602kcal**
Total Carbohydrates **47g**
Protein **32g**
Total Fat **33g**
Saturated Fat **11g**
Polyunsaturated Fat **2g**
Monounsaturated Fat **13g**
Trans Fat **2.0g**
Cholesterol **64mg**
Sodium **244mg**
Potassium **893mg**
Dietary Fiber **13g**
Sugars **11g**
Vitamin A **23% Daily Value**
Vitamin C **27% Daily Value**
Calcium **34% Daily Value**
Iron **26% Daily Value**

Tuscan Tuna Salad

Serves: 4

A delicious flavor combination celebrating all things Tuscan! What really make this tuna salad sing are the zinging pops of flavor from the capers and the peppery, earthy tones from the arugula. Unlike what you get with other salads, you will find this one is very satisfying and filling. Bursting with nutritional goodness, loaded with protein and fiber, this meal will have you feeling on top of the world and keep you going right through to the evening. The recipe is also quite versatile. Feel free to substitute other proteins, such as salmon or cooked chicken, for the tuna. You could even just increase the amount of chickpeas and omit the tuna for a vegetarian option.

INGREDIENTS

14 oz. canned tuna in water, drained

8 oz. canned chickpeas, drained and rinsed

3 cups arugula leaves

1 large tomato, seeded and diced

1 small/medium cucumber, halved lengthwise and sliced

½ cup thinly sliced red onion

⅓ cup sliced olives

2 tbsp. capers

2 tbsp. chopped fresh basil leaves

¼ cup Italian dressing

INSTRUCTIONS

1. Combine all the ingredients except the dressing in a bowl. Add the Italian dressing and lightly toss together.
2. Divide among serving bowls and serve immediately.

NUTRITION DATA FOR 1 SERVING:

Calories **262kcal**	Sodium **983mg**
Total Carbohydrates **21g**	Potassium **605mg**
Protein **29g**	Dietary Fiber **4g**
Total Fat **7g**	Sugars **5g**
Saturated Fat **1g**	Vitamin A **19% Daily Value**
Polyunsaturated Fat **3g**	Vitamin C **22% Daily Value**
Monounsaturated Fat **2g**	Calcium **8% Daily Value**
Trans Fat **0.5g**	Iron **18% Daily Value**
Cholesterol **30mg**	

Serves: 4

There are times when a salad just won't do for lunch. Those times call for this Tuscan Sausage & Bean Soup. Soup is a great option that can be made ahead of time and transported easily if you're eating lunch away from home. This comforting, hearty and nourishing meal is bursting with flavor, mainly thanks to the addition of Italian sausage and fresh basil. Perfect for when the weather is cool, this soup will warm your heart—an excellent comfort food, indeed.

Tuscan Sausage & Bean Soup

INGREDIENTS

3 mild Italian sausages, sliced ½ inch thick

14 oz. canned cannellini beans, drained and rinsed

2 celery stalks, sliced

1 large zucchini, sliced

1 large carrot, sliced

1 medium onion, peeled and diced

3 cups beef stock

8 oz. tomato puree

3 tbsp. chopped fresh basil

salt and pepper, to taste

½ cup freshly grated Parmesan cheese

INSTRUCTIONS

1. Heat a large saucepan over medium-high heat. Add the sliced sausages and cook until browned on all sides, about 8-12 minutes, then drain off any excess fat.

2. Add the beans, celery, zucchini, carrot and onion and cook, stirring, for 2 minutes.

3. Add the beef stock, tomato puree and basil and mix thoroughly.

4. Bring to a boil, then reduce the heat to low and allow to simmer, uncovered, for approximately 30 minutes, or until the soup has thickened and the vegetables are tender.

5. Season with salt and pepper, to taste.

6. Ladle into bowls and garnish with grated Parmesan cheese.

NUTRITION DATA FOR 1 SERVING:

Calories **443kcal**	Monounsaturated Fat **9g**	Sugars **9g**
Total Carbohydrates **39g**	Trans Fat **1.3g**	Vitamin A **108% Daily Value**
Protein **25g**	Cholesterol **43mg**	Vitamin C **49% Daily Value**
Total Fat **22g**	Sodium **2070mg**	Calcium **22% Daily Value**
Saturated Fat **8g**	Potassium **1303mg**	Iron **26% Daily Value**
Polyunsaturated Fat **3g**	Dietary Fiber **8g**	

Dinner

RECIPES

Mediterranean Baked Cod with Lemon & Garlic

Serves: 4

This Mediterranean staple recipe can be whipped up in just over 20 minutes. A handful of Mediterranean spices plus a mixture of lemon juice, olive oil and garlic give it a glorious flavor!

INGREDIENTS

¼ cup plus 1 tbsp. fresh lemon juice

5 tbsp extra-virgin olive oil

2 tbsp. butter, melted

⅓ cup all-purpose flour

1 tsp. ground coriander

⅓ tsp. sweet Spanish paprika

⅓ tsp. ground cumin

⅓ tsp. salt

½ tsp. black pepper

1½ lb. cod fillets (4–6 pieces)

5 cloves garlic, minced

¼ cup chopped fresh parsley leaves

INSTRUCTIONS

1. Preheat the oven to 400°F. In a shallow bowl, combine the lemon juice, 3 tablespoons of olive oil, and melted butter. Set aside.

2. In another shallow bowl, combine the all-purpose flour, coriander, paprika, cumin, salt and pepper.

3. Pat the fish fillets dry. Dip each fillet in the lemon juice mixture, then dip in the flour mixture. Shake off excess flour and set the fillets aside in a single layer (not touching one another). Reserve the remaining lemon juice mixture.

4. Heat the remaining 2 tablespoons of olive oil in a cast iron skillet over medium-high heat. When the oil is shimmering, but not smoking, add the fish and sear on each side just enough to give it some color, about 4 minutes per side. It will not be fully cooked. Remove from the heat.

5. Add the minced garlic to the reserved lemon juice mixture and mix. Drizzle all over the fish fillets.

6. Transfer the skillet to the oven and bake for 10 minutes, until the fish begins to flake easily with a fork. Remove from the oven and sprinkle chopped parsley over the top.

7. You can serve immediately with the Mediterranean Chickpea Salad (page 210).

NUTRITION DATA FOR 1 SERVING:

Calories **312kcal**	Sodium **287mg**
Total Carbohydrates **16g**	Potassium **706mg**
Protein **23g**	Dietary Fiber **7g**
Total Fat **18g**	Sugars **2g**
Saturated Fat **2g**	Vitamin A **4% Daily Value**
Polyunsaturated Fat **10g**	Vitamin C **1% Daily Value**
Monounsaturated Fat **5g**	Calcium **18% Daily Value**
Trans Fat **0g**	Iron **4% Daily Value**
Cholesterol **40mg**	

Serves: 6

You don't need a special rotisserie to make this simple homemade shawarma chicken recipe! Chicken pieces are tossed in spices of the Middle East, then baked until perfectly tender. Serve in pita pockets with Mediterranean salad and sauces.

Chicken Shawarma

INGREDIENTS

FOR THE CHICKEN:

⅓ tbsp. ground cumin

⅓ tbsp. ground turmeric

⅓ tbsp. ground coriander

⅓ tbsp. garlic powder

⅓ tbsp. paprika

½ tsp. ground cloves

½ tsp. cayenne pepper, or more to taste

8 boneless, skinless chicken thighs

1 tsp. salt

1 large onion, thinly sliced

1 large lemon, juiced

⅓ cup extra-virgin olive oil

INSTRUCTIONS

1. In a small bowl, combine the cumin, turmeric, coriander, garlic powder, paprika, cloves and cayenne pepper. Set aside the shawarma spice mix.

2. Pat the chicken thighs dry and season them with salt on both sides, then thinly slice into small bite-sized pieces.

3. Transfer the sliced chicken to a large bowl. Add the shawarma spices and toss to coat. Add the onions, lemon juice and olive oil. Toss everything together again.

4. Cover tightly and refrigerate for 3 hours or overnight. If you lack time, you can skip this step or reduce the time by half.

5. Once everything is ready, preheat your oven to 425°F. Remove the chicken from the fridge and let it sit at room temperature for a few minutes.

6. Spread the marinated chicken with the onions in a single layer on a large, lightly oiled baking sheet. Roast for 30 minutes.

TO SERVE:

6 pita pockets

Tahini Sauce (page 202) or Smooth Tzatziki (page 200)

baby arugula

pickles or kalamata olives (optional)

7. To get a more browned, crispier chicken, move the pan to the top rack and broil very briefly, 2–3 minutes. Remove the chicken from the oven.

8. To serve, open the pita pockets up. Add a little tzatziki sauce and/or tahini sauce to each pocket, then add the chicken shawarma, arugula, and pickles or olives. Serve immediately!

NUTRITION DATA FOR 1 SERVING:

Calories **227kcal**	Sodium **403mg**
Total Carbohydrates **22g**	Potassium **350mg**
Protein **17g**	Dietary Fiber **3g**
Total Fat **15g**	Sugars **4g**
Saturated Fat **2g**	Vitamin A **1% Daily Value**
Polyunsaturated Fat **6g**	Vitamin C **3% Daily Value**
Monounsaturated Fat **5g**	Calcium **22% Daily Value**
Trans Fat **0g**	Iron **8% Daily Value**
Cholesterol **64.6mg**	

Moroccan Vegetable Tagine

Serves: 6

This simple tagine recipe is full of warm Moroccan flavors and is one of my favorite single-pot dishes. It is an all-star, all-vegetable tagine, packed with the perfect balance of Moroccan flavors, and it's vegan and gluten-free!

INGREDIENTS

¼ cup extra-virgin olive oil, plus more for serving

2 medium yellow onions, peeled and chopped

2 large carrots, peeled and chopped

2 large russet potatoes, peeled and cubed

1 large sweet potato, peeled and cubed

8–10 cloves garlic, peeled and chopped

1 tsp. salt

1 tbsp. harissa spice blend

1 tsp. ground coriander

1 tsp. ground cinnamon

½ tsp. ground turmeric

2 cups canned tomatoes, chopped

heaping ½ cup chopped dried apricots

1 quart low-sodium vegetable broth (or broth of your choice)

2 cups cooked chickpeas

1 lemon, juiced

handful of fresh parsley leaves

INSTRUCTIONS

1. In a medium pot or Dutch oven, heat the olive oil over medium heat until it is just shimmering. Add the onions and increase the heat to medium-high. Sauté for 5 minutes, tossing regularly.

2. Add the carrots, russet potatoes, sweet potato, and garlic. Season with the salt and spices and toss to combine evenly. Cook for 5 to 7 minutes, mixing regularly with a wooden spoon.

3. Add the tomatoes, apricots and broth. Season again with just a small dash more salt.

4. Cook for 10 minutes, keeping the heat on medium-high. Then reduce the heat to low, cover and simmer for another 20 to 25 minutes, or until the veggies are tender.

5. Stir in the chickpeas and cook another 5 minutes. Stir in the lemon juice and fresh parsley. Taste and adjust the seasoning, adding more salt or harissa spice blend according to your preference.

6. Transfer the tagine to serving bowls and top each serving with a generous drizzle of extra-virgin olive oil. Serve hot with your favorite bread, couscous or rice. Enjoy!

NUTRITION DATA FOR 1 SERVING:

Calories **448kcal**	Sodium **405mg**
Total Carbohydrates **60g**	Potassium **785mg**
Protein **16g**	Dietary Fiber **8g**
Total Fat **18g**	Sugars **22.5g**
Saturated Fat **2g**	Vitamin A **4% Daily Value**
Polyunsaturated Fat **8g**	Vitamin C **8% Daily Value**
Monounsaturated Fat **4g**	Calcium **28% Daily Value**
Trans Fat **4g**	Iron **10% Daily Value**
Cholesterol **2mg**	

Seafood Paella

Serves: 6

Here's a simple, saffron-infused paella recipe with lobster and shrimp. You don't need a special paella pan—a large, solid skillet like cast-iron will work well.

Plus, there's no need to wait for a special opportunity—this recipe will deliver the *wow* factor on any night!

INGREDIENTS

3 cups water

4 small lobster tails (6–12 oz. each)

3 tbsp. extra-virgin olive oil

1 large yellow onion, chopped

2 cups Spanish rice or medium-grain rice, soaked in water for 20 minutes, then drained

4 cloves garlic, chopped

2 large pinches Spanish saffron threads, soaked in ½ cup water

1 tsp. sweet Spanish paprika

1 tsp. cayenne pepper

½ tsp. Aleppo pepper (or other chili pepper flakes)

1 tsp. salt

2 large Roma tomatoes, finely chopped

6 oz. French green beans, trimmed

1 lb. prawns or large shrimp of your choice, peeled and deveined

¼ cup chopped fresh parsley

INSTRUCTIONS

1. In a large saucepan, bring the 3 cups of water to a boil. Add the lobster tails and boil gently 1–2 minutes, until pink. Turn the heat off. With a pair of tongs, remove the lobster tails and set aside to cool. Do not discard the lobster cooking water. When the lobster is cool enough to handle, remove and discard the shells and cut the lobster into large chunks.

2. In a large, deep pan or cast-iron skillet, heat the olive oil over medium-high heat. Add the onions and sauté for 2 minutes, then add the rice. Cook for 3 more minutes, stirring regularly. Add the chopped garlic and the lobster cooking water. Stir in the saffron and its soaking liquid, and the paprika, cayenne pepper, Aleppo pepper and salt.

3. Stir in the tomatoes and green beans. Bring to a boil for 10 minutes to let the liquid slightly reduce, then turn down the heat to low, cover and cook for 20 minutes.

4. Uncover and spread the shrimp over the rice, slightly pushing it into the rice. Add a little water if you need to. Cover and cook for another 10 minutes or until the shrimp turns pink. Finally, add the cooked lobster chunks. When the lobster is warmed through, turn off the heat. Garnish with parsley.

5. Serve the paella hot and enjoy!

NUTRITION DATA FOR 1 SERVING:

Calories **516kcal**	Sodium **507mg**
Total Carbohydrates **61g**	Potassium **403mg**
Protein **41g**	Dietary Fiber **3g**
Total Fat **21g**	Sugars **0g**
Saturated Fat **10g**	Vitamin A **10% Daily Value**
Polyunsaturated Fat **4g**	Vitamin C **4% Daily Value**
Monounsaturated Fat **5g**	Calcium **41% Daily Value**
Trans Fat **2g**	Iron **17% Daily Value**
Cholesterol **12mg**	

Traditional Greek Roasted Vegetables (Briam)

Serves: 6

This is the perfect opportunity to get your Greek on! Briam is a simple and absolutely delicious roasted vegetable dish, prepared in the Greek style. Stir the potatoes, zucchini and red onion in a mixture of extra-virgin olive oil, garlic, parsley and spices, then roast with the chopped tomatoes. You'll end up with a healthy, vegan Mediterranean dish that can be served as a main entrée or alongside other dishes.

INGREDIENTS

1¼ lb. gold potatoes (about 3 medium-size potatoes), peeled and thinly sliced into rounds about ⅛-inch thick

1¼ lb. zucchini squash (2 to 3 zucchini), thinly sliced into rounds about ¼ inch thick

1 tsp. kosher salt

1 tsp. black pepper

2 tsp. dried oregano

scant 1 tsp. dried rosemary

½ cup chopped fresh parsley

4 cloves garlic, minced

2 tbsp. extra-virgin olive oil, plus more for serving

1 (28-oz.) can diced tomatoes with juice (preferably no-salt-added organic tomatoes)

1 large red onion or 2 smaller red onions, thinly sliced into rounds (if large, you'll want to cut the onion in half first, then slice)

INSTRUCTIONS

1. Preheat the oven to 400°F. Arrange a rack in the middle.

2. Place the sliced potatoes and zucchini in a large mixing bowl. Season with the salt, pepper, oregano and rosemary. Add the fresh parsley, garlic and a generous drizzle of extra-virgin olive oil. Toss and mix to make sure the vegetables are well coated with the oil and spices.

3. On a baking pan or in a very large, oven-safe skillet, spread half of the canned diced tomatoes to cover the bottom of the pan.

4. Arrange the seasoned potatoes and zucchini and the sliced onions in the pan, working in rows and alternating the veggies in a pattern.

5. If you have any oil-garlic mixture left in the mixing bowl, pour that all over the veggies, then top with the remaining diced tomatoes.

6. Cover the pan with foil, making sure it's not touching the veggies. Bake for 45 minutes. Take the pan out briefly to carefully remove the foil, then place back in the oven, uncovered, and roast for another 30 to 40 minutes, or until the veggies are soft and charred and most of the liquid has evaporated.

7. Remove from the oven. Add a generous drizzle of extra-virgin olive oil and serve warm or at room temperature.

NUTRITION DATA FOR 1 SERVING:

Calories **68kcal**	Sodium **13mg**
Total Carbohydrates **10g**	Potassium **18mg**
Protein **2g**	Dietary Fiber **6g**
Total Fat **6g**	Sugars **3g**
Saturated Fat **2g**	Vitamin A **6% Daily Value**
Polyunsaturated Fat **3g**	Vitamin C **8% Daily Value**
Monounsaturated Fat **2g**	Calcium **47% Daily Value**
Trans Fat **0g**	Iron **16% Daily Value**
Cholesterol **0mg**	

Kofta Kebab

Makes:
10 skewers

This is an authentic, must-try recipe for Kofta Kebab: ground beef and lamb mixed with fresh parsley, onion, garlic and Middle Eastern spices. These kebabs will feed a crowd, and you can serve many sides and salads with them.

INGREDIENTS

1 medium yellow onion, quartered

2 cloves garlic

1 bunch parsley, stems removed (about 2 packed cups parsley leaves), plus more for serving

1 lb. ground beef

½ lb. ground lamb

1 slice bread, toasted until browned and soaked in water until fully toft

1 tsp. salt

1 tsp. black pepper

1½ tsp. ground allspice

½ tsp. cayenne pepper

½ tsp. ground green cardamom

½ tsp. ground sumac

½ tsp. ground nutmeg

½ tsp. paprika

FOR SERVING:

pita bread

Tahini Sauce (page 202)

tomato wedges

onion wedges

INSTRUCTIONS

1. Begin by soaking 10 wooden skewers in water for 30 minutes to 1 hour. Take them out of the water when you are ready to begin. Lightly oil the grates of a gas grill and preheat to medium-high for about 20 minutes. Prepare the pita bread and fixings and any other sides before you begin grilling.

2. In a food processor, chop the onion, garlic and parsley.

3. Add the beef and lamb. Squeeze all the water out of the bread and add to the food processor, then add all the spices. Run the processor until the ingredients are well combined and form a pasty mixture.

4. Transfer the meat mixture to a large bowl. Take a fistful of the mixture and mold it onto a wooden skewer to create a kebab about 1 inch thick. Set the skewered kebab on a parchment paper–lined tray. Repeat the process until you have no meat left.

5. Place the kebabs on the grill. Grill for 4 minutes on one side, then turn over and grill for another 3 to 4 minutes.

6. Serve your kofta kebabs immediately with pita bread, tahini, and tomato and onion wedges.

NUTRITION DATA FOR 1 SERVING:

Calories **197kcal**	Sodium **1178mg**
Total Carbohydrates **3g**	Potassium **314mg**
Protein **18g**	Dietary Fiber **1g**
Total Fat **12g**	Sugars **0g**
Saturated Fat **5g**	Vitamin A **3% Daily Value**
Polyunsaturated Fat **2g**	Vitamin C **9% Daily Value**
Monounsaturated Fat **4g**	Calcium **31% Daily Value**
Trans Fat **1g**	Iron **10% Daily Value**
Cholesterol **63mg**	

Serves: 6

This tasty roast chicken is seasoned with a simple blend of spices along with fresh garlic and olive oil, and finished with parsley and fresh basil. You'll love this healthy and juicy Italian chicken recipe.

Rosemary Baked Chicken

INGREDIENTS

2 lb. boneless, skinless chicken breasts

1 tsp. salt

1 tsp. black pepper

2 tsp. dried oregano

1 tsp. fresh thyme leaves (from about 2 sprigs thyme)

1 tsp. sweet paprika

4 cloves garlic, minced

3 tbsp. extra-virgin olive oil, plus more for the pan

½ lemon, juiced

1 medium red onion, halved and thinly sliced

5 to 6 Campari tomatoes (or small Roma tomatoes), halved

handful fresh parsley, chopped for garnish

fresh basil leaves, for garnish

fresh rosemary leaves, chopped for garnish

INSTRUCTIONS

1. Preheat the oven to 375°F.

2. Pat the chicken dry. Place the chicken breasts in a large zip-top bag, remove any air from the bag and seal the top, and set the bag on a cutting board. Pound the chicken with a meat mallet to flatten to about ¼ inch thick. Remove the chicken from the zip-top bag and set aside. Reuse the bag and mallet to repeat the process with the remaining chicken breast pieces.

3. Season the chicken with salt and pepper on both sides and place in a large bowl or dish. Add the spices, garlic, olive oil and lemon juice. Combine to make sure the chicken is evenly coated.

4. Grease a baking dish or pan with olive oil, then spread the onion slices on the bottom. Arrange the seasoned chicken over the onions, and top with the tomatoes.

5. Cover the baking dish tightly with foil and bake for 10 minutes, then uncover and bake another 8–10 minutes. Watch carefully because the cooking time will vary depending on the thickness of your chicken breasts. To be sure the chicken is cooked through, use a digital instant-read or meat thermometer to check for the proper internal temperature of 165°F.

6. Remove the chicken from the oven, cover with foil or another pan and let rest 5–10 minutes. Uncover and garnish with fresh parsley, basil and rosemary. Serve and enjoy!

NUTRITION DATA FOR 1 SERVING:

Calories **290kcal**
Total Carbohydrates **11g**
Protein **35.9g**
Total Fat **11.5g**
Saturated Fat **2g**
Polyunsaturated Fat **1g**
Monounsaturated Fat **6g**
Trans Fat **2.5g**
Cholesterol **51 mg**
Sodium **272.5mg**
Potassium **124.6mg**
Dietary Fiber **2g**
Sugars **5g**
Vitamin A **7% Daily Value**
Vitamin C **15% Daily Value**
Calcium **18% Daily Value**
Iron **21% Daily Value**

Moroccan Lamb Stew

Serves: 7

If you want to make the best lamb stew, this recipe is all you need! Comforting, tender lamb is braised with lots of vegetables, chickpeas and warm Moroccan flavors. Serve with couscous!

INGREDIENTS

2 tbsp. extra-virgin olive oil, plus more as needed

1 large yellow onion, chopped

3 carrots, chopped

6 Yukon Gold potatoes (or any small potatoes), peeled and ½-inch cubed

3 large cloves garlic, roughly chopped

1½ tsp. kosher salt

1½ tsp. black pepper

2.5 lb. boneless leg of lamb, fat trimmed, cut into cubes (or boneless lamb shoulder, fat trimmed)

½ cup dried apricots

1 cinnamon stick

1 bay leaf

1½ tsp. ground allspice

1½ tsp. Moroccan spice, such as ras el hanout

½ tsp. ground ginger

6 canned, peeled plum tomatoes, halved

2½ cups low-sodium beef broth

1 (15-oz.) can chickpeas

INSTRUCTIONS

1. Preheat the oven to 350°F.

2. In a medium Dutch oven, heat the olive oil over medium heat until shimmering.

3. Add the onions, carrots and potatoes and sauté for 4 minutes. Add garlic and cook for an additional 3 minutes and season with salt and pepper. Transfer the vegetables to a plate and set aside.

4. Add the lamb to the same pot, adding more oil if needed, and cook until deeply brown on all sides, about 8–12 minutes. Season with salt and pepper.

5. Adjust the heat to medium-high and return the sautéed vegetables to the pot. Add the dried apricots, cinnamon stick, bay leaf, allspice, moroccan spice and ginger and stir to coat.

6. Add the plum tomatoes and broth and bring everything to a boil for 5 minutes.

7. Cover the pot and place in the oven for 1½ hours (check partway through to see if more water or broth is needed). Stir in the chickpeas, cover and return to the oven for another 30 minutes.

8. Remove from the oven and serve hot with your choice of rice, couscous, pita bread or your favorite rustic bread.

NUTRITION DATA FOR 1 SERVING:

Calories **431kcal**	Sodium **167 mg**
Total Carbohydrates **56g**	Potassium **96mg**
Protein **37g**	Dietary Fiber **3g**
Total Fat **8g**	Sugars **8g**
Saturated Fat **2g**	Vitamin A **4% Daily Value**
Polyunsaturated Fat **4g**	Vitamin C **18% Daily Value**
Monounsaturated Fat **1g**	Calcium **31% Daily Value**
Trans Fat **2g**	Iron **29% Daily Value**
Cholesterol **48mg**	

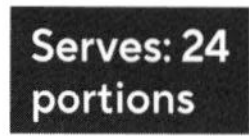
Serves: 24 portions

Are you ready to learn how to make Authentic Falafel from scratch? This is a family recipe for the best authentic falafel, made from chickpeas, fresh herbs and all the right spices.

There are so many ways to enjoy this falafel: in a sandwich with tahini sauce or hummus, on a platter with Mediterranean tomato and cucumber salad, or alongside other dishes as a side. Experiment to find your favorite!

Authentic Falafel

INGREDIENTS

2 cups dried chickpeas (do not use canned or cooked chickpeas)

½ tsp. baking soda

1 cup fresh parsley

⅓ cup fresh cilantro leaves

½ cup fresh dill fronds

1 small onion, quartered

7–8 cloves garlic, peeled

salt, to taste

1 tbsp. ground black pepper

1 tbsp. ground cumin

1 tbsp. ground coriander

1 tsp. cayenne pepper (optional)

1 tsp. baking powder

2 tbsp. toasted sesame seeds

canola oil for frying

INSTRUCTIONS

A DAY AHEAD:

1. Combine the dried chickpeas and baking soda in a large bowl and fill with water to cover the chickpeas by at least 2 inches.

2. Soak for at least 18 hours, or longer if the chickpeas are still very hard.

WHEN READY TO MAKE THE FALAFEL:

3. Drain the chickpeas completely and pat them dry. Transfer to the large bowl of a food processor fitted with the chopping blade.

4. Add the herbs, onions, garlic, salt, pepper, cumin, coriander, and cayenne pepper, if using, to the chickpeas. Run the food processor 40 seconds at a time until the falafel mixture is well combined.

5. Transfer the falafel mixture to a container and cover tightly. Refrigerate for at least 1 hour or a maximum of 24 hours.

WHEN READY TO COOK:

6. Add the baking powder and sesame seeds to the falafel mixture and stir with a spoon.

7. Scoop tablespoonfuls of the falafel mixture and form into ½-inch-thick patties. It helps to have wet hands as you form the patties.

8. Fill up a medium saucepan 3 inches with oil. Heat the oil over medium-high until it

Tahini Paste
(page 204)

TO SERVE AS SANDWICHES (OPTIONAL):

12 pita pockets

hummus

English cucumbers, chopped or diced

tomatoes, chopped or diced

baby arugula

pickles

bubbles softly. Working in batches if necessary, you should carefully drop the falafel patties in the oil and let them fry for 3 to 5 minutes, until crispy and medium brown on the outside. Do not crowd the falafel in the saucepan.

9. Place the fried falafel patties in a colander or on a plate lined with paper towels to drain. Repeat with the remaining patties.

10. Serve the falafel hot next to other small plates with the sauce drizzles over. Or serve the patties in the falafel pita pockets with tahini or hummus, cucumbers, tomatoes, arugula and pickles if desired. Enjoy!

NUTRITION DATA FOR 1 SERVING:

Calories **93kcal**	Sodium **13mg**
Total Carbohydrates **1g**	Potassium **99mg**
Protein **4g**	Dietary Fiber **4g**
Total Fat **4g**	Sugars **2g**
Saturated Fat **0.4g**	Vitamin A **6% Daily Value**
Polyunsaturated Fat **1g**	Vitamin C **14% Daily Value**
Monounsaturated Fat **2g**	Calcium **21% Daily Value**
Trans Fat **1g**	Iron **17% Daily Value**
Cholesterol **34mg**	

Shakshuka with Tomato Sauce & Pepper

Serves: 6

This simple shakshuka is made from eggs that are lightly poached in a mixture of simmering tomatoes, peppers, onions and garlic. A few warm spices and some fresh herbs complete the satisfying one-skillet dish. Serve for breakfast, lunch or dinner!

INGREDIENTS

3 tbsp. extra-virgin olive oil

1 large yellow onion, chopped

2 green bell peppers, chopped

2 cloves garlic, peeled and chopped

1 tsp. ground coriander

1 tsp. sweet paprika

½ tsp. ground cumin

salt and pepper, to taste

6 vine-ripe tomatoes, chopped (about 6 cups chopped tomatoes)

½ cup tomato sauce

6 large eggs

¼ cup chopped fresh parsley

¼ cup chopped fresh mint

pinch of red pepper flakes (optional)

INSTRUCTIONS

1. In a large skillet, heat the olive oil over medium heat. Add the onions, peppers, garlic, spices and a pinch each of salt and pepper. Cook, stirring occasionally, until the vegetables have softened, about 5 minutes.

2. Add the tomatoes and tomato sauce. Cover and let simmer for about 15 minutes. Uncover and cook a bit longer to allow the mixture to reduce and thicken, then taste and adjust the seasoning to your liking.

3. Use a wooden spoon to create 6 wells in the tomato mixture, making sure the indentations are well spaced out. Gently crack an egg into each well.

4. Lower the heat, cover the skillet, and cook on low until the egg whites are set, about 3–5 minutes.

5. Uncover and add the fresh parsley and mint. You can add more black pepper or crushed red pepper, if you prefer. Serve with warm pita, challah bread or your choice of crusty bread.

NUTRITION DATA FOR 1 SERVING:

Calories **154kcal**	Sodium **86mg**
Total Carbohydrates **14g**	Potassium **100mg**
Protein **9g**	Dietary Fiber **34g**
Total Fat **8g**	Sugars **1g**
Saturated Fat **4g**	Vitamin A **3% Daily Value**
Polyunsaturated Fat **2g**	Vitamin C **18% Daily Value**
Monounsaturated Fat **1g**	Calcium **45% Daily Value**
Trans Fat **1g**	Iron **12% Daily Value**
Cholesterol **192mg**	

Serves: 5

You'll love this simple homemade Greek chicken gyro recipe: pita wraps filled with yogurt-marinated chicken, packed in the flavor of warm spices, with homemade tzatziki sauce and all the extras you love! Here we cook the Greek chicken in a nonstick skillet, but you can also make it on an outdoor grill or in the oven.

Chicken Gyro

INGREDIENTS

FOR THE CHICKEN:

1.5 lb. chicken breast

1 cup plain Greek yogurt (you can use reduced-fat or fat-free Greek yogurt if you like)

3 tbsp. extra-virgin olive oil, divided

1 large lemon, juiced

2 tbsp. red wine vinegar

3 garlic cloves, minced

1 tbsp. dried oregano

1 tsp. sweet paprika

1 tsp. ground cumin

1 tsp. ground coriander

generous pinch kosher salt

generous pinch ground black pepper

pinch cayenne pepper (optional)

INSTRUCTIONS

1. First, marinate the chicken. In a big mixing bowl, combine the yogurt, 1 tbsp. of the olive oil, the red wine vinegar, garlic, oregano, paprika, cumin, coriander, salt, pepper and cayenne, if using, and mix well. Add the chicken and mix to make sure each piece is well coated with the marinade. Cover and refrigerate for at least 30 minutes, or overnight.

2. When ready to cook, heat the remaining tablespoon olive oil in a nonstick skillet over medium-high heat until shimmering but not smoking. Remove the chicken from the marinade and shake off any excess, then add the chicken to the pan. Cook undisturbed on one side for 5 minutes, until browned. Use tongs to turn the chicken over and cook on the other side for another 5 minutes or until chicken is done.

3. To assemble the chicken gyros, warm up the pita bread in the oven. Spread the tzatziki sauce on top, then add chicken and top with tomato, cucumber, green pepper, red onion and olives as you like. Squeeze the lemon over, wrap the pita up and enjoy!

TO SERVE:

5 pita bread

Smooth Tzatziki (page 200)

1 large tomato, sliced

1 cucumber, sliced

1 green pepper, cored and sliced

1 small red onion, sliced into half-moons

1 cup pitted Kalamata olives

NUTRITION DATA FOR 1 SERVING:

Calories **303kcal**	Sodium **159.8mg**
Total Carbohydrates **16.4g**	Potassium **104.6mg**
Protein **36.7g**	Dietary Fiber **2.8g**
Total Fat **10g**	Sugars **4.8g**
Polyunsaturated Fat **5g**	Vitamin A **6% Daily Value**
Monounsaturated Fat **2.6g**	Vitamin C **12% Daily Value**
Saturated Fat **1.7g**	Calcium **35% Daily Value**
Trans Fat **1.3g**	Iron **14% Daily Value**
Cholesterol **55.1mg**	

Makes:
16 pieces

If you have not tried these grilled Greek meatballs in red sauce, here is a gift for you! These are known as soutzoukakia or Izmir kofta, and they are the best!

These roasted meatballs have lots of flavor, with fresh parsley and a special blend of spices, including ground cumin, baked in a special red sauce. Plus, when you soak the bread in milk, it makes these Greek meatballs even juicier.

Sweet Baked Meatballs (Soutzoukakia)

INGREDIENTS

FOR THE MEATBALLS:

2 slices whole-wheat or gluten-free bread, toasted to a medium-brown

¼ -⅓ cup milk or water

1.5 lb. lean ground beef

1 small yellow onion, chopped

3 cloves garlic, minced

2 medium eggs

1 tsp. ground cumin

½ tsp. ground cinnamon

½ tsp. dried oregano

½ cup chopped fresh parsley, plus more for garnish

1 tbsp. salt

1 tbsp. black pepper

INSTRUCTIONS

1. Place the toasted bread in a small bowl, cover with the milk or water and set aside to soak. When bread is soft and well-soaked, squeeze the liquid out completely and discard any remaining milk.

2. Transfer the bread to a large mixing bowl. Add the ground beef, onion, garlic, eggs, cumin, cinnamon, oregano, parsley, salt and pepper. Knead until the mixture is well combined. Cover the meat mixture and let rest in the fridge while you continue on to the next step.

3. Preheat the oven to 400°F.

4. In a saucepan or large skillet, heat the olive oil over medium heat until shimmering but not smoking. Add the onions and cook for about 3 minutes, stirring often. Add the garlic and cook for another minute, stirring regularly. Add the red wine and cook to reduce by about half, about 10–12 minutes. Then add the tomato sauce, bay leaf, cumin, cinnamon, sugar, and salt and pepper, to taste. Bring to a boil, then lower the heat and simmer for 15 minutes.

5. Meanwhile, lightly grease the bottom of a large baking dish with extra-virgin olive oil.

6. Take the meat mixture out of the fridge. Wet your hands and scoop out about 2½ tablespoons

drizzle of extra-virgin olive oil, plus more for the baking dish

FOR THE RED SAUCE:

2 tbsp. extra-virgin olive oil

1 medium yellow onion, finely chopped

2 cloves garlic, minced

½ cup dry red wine

2 (15-oz.) cans tomato sauce

1 bay leaf

⅓ tsp. ground cumin

½ tsp. ground cinnamon

½ tsp. sugar

salt and black pepper, to taste

of the meat mixture, then form it into a large, football-shaped meatball. Repeat with the remaining meat mixture to create 15 to 16 elongated meatballs.

7. Arrange the meatballs in the prepared baking dish. Remove the bay leaf from the sauce and top the meatballs with the sauce.

8. Place the baking dish on the middle rack of the oven. Bake for 40 to 45 minutes or until the meatballs are well cooked all the way through (check halfway through to make sure the baking dish is not dry; if needed, add a little bit of water to the bottom of the dish).

9. Remove from the oven and add another drizzle of olive oil. Garnish with parsley and serve over rice or orzo if desired.

NUTRITION DATA FOR 1 SERVING:

Calories **64kcal**	Sodium **178mg**
Total Carbohydrate **7g**	Potassium **96mg**
Protein **2g**	Dietary Fiber **0g**
Total Fat **3g**	Sugars **3g**
Saturated Fat **5g**	Vitamin A **2% Daily Value**
Polyunsaturated Fat **2g**	Vitamin C **5% Daily Value**
Monounsaturated Fat **1g**	Calcium **25% Daily Value**
Trans Fat **2g**	Iron **16% Daily Value**
Cholesterol **29mg**	

Shrimp & Leek Spaghetti

Serves: 4

Light and lemony, this pasta provides almost a third of the daily fiber needed by your body. Thanks to prepeeled shrimp and frozen peas, it's the epitome of weeknight-fast. You can dress it up with a glass of crisp white wine.

INGREDIENTS

8 oz. whole-grain spaghetti

1 lb. medium raw shrimp, peeled and deveined

½ tsp. black pepper

½ tsp. kosher salt, divided

1½ tbsp. olive oil, divided

2 cups chopped leek (1 large leek)

3 cloves garlic

2 cups (about 9 oz.) frozen baby sweet peas

¼ cup heavy cream

2 tsp. lemon zest

2 tbsp. fresh lemon juice

2 tbsp. chopped fresh dill

INSTRUCTIONS

1. Cook the pasta according to the directions on the package, but do not salt the cooking water. Reserving ½ cup of the cooking liquid, drain the pasta, then cover to keep it warm and set aside.

2. While the pasta cooks, pat the shrimp dry with paper towels; season with the pepper and ¼ teaspoon of the salt. Heat half of the olive oil in a large nonstick skillet over high heat. Add the shrimp and cook, stirring often, until cooked through, 3 to 4 minutes. Transfer to a plate and cover to keep warm. (Do not wipe the skillet clean.)

3. Reduce the heat to medium-high. Add the leek, garlic, the remaining oil and the remaining ¼ teaspoon salt. Cook, stirring often, until the leek is slightly tender, 2 to 3 minutes. Add the peas, cream, lemon zest, lemon juice and the reserved ½ cup of the cooking liquid. Reduce the heat to medium and simmer until the sauce thickens slightly, 2 to 3 minutes. Return the shrimp to the skillet and toss to coat.

4. Divide the pasta among 4 bowls and top evenly with the shrimp and sauce. Sprinkle with dill and serve immediately.

NUTRITION DATA FOR 1 SERVING:

Calories **446kcal**	Sodium **649mg**
Total Carbohydrates **59g**	Potassium **454mg**
Protein **28g**	Dietary Fiber **9g**
Total Fat **13g**	Sugars **8g**
Saturated Fat **5g**	Vitamin A **7% Daily Value**
Polyunsaturated Fat **3g**	Vitamin C **4% Daily Value**
Monounsaturated Fat **4g**	Calcium **14% Daily Value**
Trans Fat **1g**	Iron **16% Daily Value**
Cholesterol **25mg**	

Panko Salmon with Snap Peas

Serves: 4

The fresh tarragon kicks this simple and elegant main dish up a notch. It has a sweet flavor that integrates the beauty of Dijon mustard. Be sure to sear the salmon fillets with the crusted side down first—they will be easier to flip once they're crisp and golden.

INGREDIENTS

1½ tbsp. Dijon mustard

1½ tbsp. mayonnaise

½ tsp. kosher salt, divided

½ tsp. black pepper, divided

4 (6-oz.) skinless salmon fillets

½ cup whole-wheat panko (Japanese bread crumbs)

1 tbsp. chopped fresh tarragon, divided

2 tsp. grated lemon rind, divided

2 tbsp. olive oil, divided

2½ cups sugar snap peas

⅓ cup thinly sliced shallots (about 2 medium)

2 tsp. fresh lemon juice

INSTRUCTIONS

1. In a shallow bowl, combine the mustard, mayonnaise, ¼ teaspoon of the salt and ¼ teaspoon of the pepper. Spoon the mustard mixture evenly over the salmon fillets. In a separate small bowl, combine the panko, 1½ teaspoons of the tarragon and 1 teaspoon of the lemon rind. Sprinkle the panko mixture over the mustard-coated side of the fillet, pressing to adhere.

2. Heat 1 tablespoon of the oil in a large nonstick skillet over medium heat. Carefully add the fillets, panko side down, to the pan. Cook 3 to 4 minutes or until golden, then turn and cook on the other side, 3 to 4 minutes, or to your desired degree of doneness. Remove the fillets from the pan; keep warm in foil.

3. Increase the heat to medium-high and add the remaining 1 tablespoon oil to the pan. Add the snap peas and shallots and cook, stirring occasionally, for 3 minutes. Add the remaining ¼ teaspoon salt, ¼ teaspoon pepper, 1½ teaspoons tarragon, 1 teaspoon lemon rind and the lemon juice. Cook for 2 minutes or until the snap peas are crisp-tender. Serve alongside the salmon fillets.

NUTRITION DATA FOR 1 SERVING:

Calories **387kcal**	Sodium **630mg**
Total Carbohydrate **13g**	Potassium **245mg**
Protein **39g**	Dietary Fiber **3g**
Total Fat **18g**	Sugars **3g**
Saturated Fat **3g**	Vitamin A **6% Daily Value**
Polyunsaturated Fat **10g**	Vitamin C **2% Daily Value**
Monounsaturated Fat **4g**	Calcium **4% Daily Value**
Trans Fat **1g**	Iron **8% Daily Value**
Cholesterol **34mg**	

Grilled Salmon with Tomato-Avocado Salsa

Serves: 4

Here we combine two ingredients from the early summer—cherry tomatoes and fresh basil—into a fresh take on salsa. For the crispiest salmon skin, make sure that your barbecue grates are very clean and that you've preheated the grill for at least 15 minutes. Avocado adds creaminess and uniquely healthy prebiotics to this recipe.

INGREDIENTS

- 2 cups diced avocado
- 1 cup halved yellow heirloom cherry tomatoes
- 2 tbsp. chopped fresh cilantro
- ½ tsp. chopped serrano chili
- 1½ tbsp. sliced shallot
- 1 tsp. fresh lime juice
- 1 tsp. kosher salt
- ⅓ tsp. black pepper
- 1 tbsp. olive oil, divided
- 4 (6-oz.) salmon fillets, skin on

INSTRUCTIONS

1. Preheat the grill to medium-high (about 450°F).

2. In a medium bowl, combine the avocado, tomatoes, cilantro, serrano chili and shallots. In a small bowl, whisk together the lime juice, ¼ teaspoon of the salt, and ¼ teaspoon of the pepper; drizzle over the avocado mixture and stir to coat.

3. Brush the olive oil on both sides of the salmon, then sprinkle with the remaining ¾ teaspoon salt and ½ teaspoon pepper.

4. Place the salmon skin side down on the grill and cook, flipping once, until the salmon is opaque and cooked through, about 3 minutes per side. Serve the salmon topped with the salsa.

NUTRITION DATA FOR 1 SERVING:

Calories **408kcal**	Sodium **574mg**
Total Carbohydrates **9g**	Potassium **367mg**
Protein **38g**	Dietary Fiber **6g**
Total Fat **24g**	Sugars **1g**
Saturated Fat **4g**	Vitamin A **2% Daily Value**
Polyunsaturated Fat **14g**	Vitamin C **5% Daily Value**
Monounsaturated Fat **5g**	Calcium **3% Daily Value**
Trans Fat **1g**	Iron **7% Daily Value**
Cholesterol **48mg**	

Serves: 4

This vegetable-filled pasta is beautiful and filling, thanks to the meaty eggplants. If you can't find burrata, simply cut 6 ounces of fresh mozzarella into small pieces.

Heading to a potluck? Feel free to make this recipe in advance— just be sure to let it come to room temperature and add an extra drop of vinegar and oil before serving. Don't forget a few tablespoons of chopped fresh basil leaves for a special layer of flavor.

Pasta Salad with Tomatoes and Eggplant

INGREDIENTS

8 oz. casarecce, fusilli or penne pasta

8 oz. haricots verts (French green beans) or yellow wax beans

1 tbsp. olive oil

2 cups chopped Japanese eggplant (1 eggplant)

1 tbsp. minced garlic

2 pints cherry tomatoes, halved and divided

¼ cup dry white wine

2 tsp. white wine vinegar

½ tsp. kosher salt

6 oz. burrata

2 tsp. chopped fresh thyme

½ tsp. black pepper

INSTRUCTIONS

1. Cook the pasta according to the package instructions, but do not salt the cooking water. Add the green beans during the last 3 minutes of cooking. Reserve 1 cup of the cooking liquid, then drain.

2. Meanwhile, heat the oil in a large skillet over medium-high heat. Add the eggplant and cook, stirring occasionally, until tender, 4 to 5 minutes. Add the garlic and cook until fragrant, 1 minute. Add half of the tomatoes and cook until their juices start to release, 2 to 3 minutes.

3. Add the wine and cook, stirring often, until most of the wine evaporates, about 3-4 minutes. Add the pasta and green beans; toss to combine. If the mixture is too dry, add the reserved pasta cooking liquid a couple of tablespoons at a time. Stir in the remaining tomatoes and the vinegar and salt. Divide the pasta mixture among 4 bowls. Top each bowl evenly with the burrata, thyme and pepper.

NUTRITION DATA FOR 1 SERVING:

Calories **428kcal**	Monounsaturated Fat **2g**	Sugars **9g**
Total Carbohydrates **56g**	Trans Fat **0g**	Vitamin A **4% Daily Value**
Protein **17g**	Cholesterol **46mg**	Vitamin C **7% Daily Value**
Total Fat **14g**	Sodium **361mg**	Calcium **28% Daily Value**
Saturated Fat **7g**	Potassium **282mg**	Iron **13% Daily Value**
Polyunsaturated Fat **5g**	Dietary Fiber **6g**	

Grilled Heirloom Tomato & Feta Panzanella

Serves: 4

Spring is the time for heirloom tomatoes—their rich flavor and vibrant color add a big wow factor to this salad. Beans increase its fiber and protein content.

INGREDIENTS

2 lb. heirloom tomatoes, halved

4 oz. French bread, cut into 1-inch slices

¼ cup extra-virgin olive oil, divided

1 (3-oz.) block feta cheese

¼ tsp. kosher salt

¼ tsp. black pepper

1 (14.5-oz.) can unsalted cannellini beans, rinsed and drained

½ cup thinly sliced red onion

½ cup chopped fresh basil leaves

2 tsp. red wine vinegar

INSTRUCTIONS

1. Preheat the grill to 450°F. Brush the tomatoes and bread with 1 tablespoon of the oil. Place the tomatoes, bread and feta cheese directly on the grates and grill until carmalized on both sides, 1 to 2 minutes per side. Transfer to a plate and sprinkle evenly with the salt and pepper. Let cool for 5 minutes, then cut any of the larger tomatoes and the bread slices into chunks.

2. Combine the tomatoes, bread, beans, onion, basil, vinegar and the remaining 3 tablespoons of oil in a large bowl; gently toss. Divide the salad among 4 plates and crumble the feta cheese evenly over the top. Serve immediately.

NUTRITION DATA FOR 1 SERVING:

Calories **381kcal**	Sodium **530mg**
Total Carbohydrates **39g**	Potassium **436mg**
Protein **13g**	Dietary Fiber **8g**
Total Fat **21g**	Sugars **10g**
Saturated Fat **5g**	Vitamin A **4% Daily Value**
Polyunsaturated Fat **11g**	Vitamin C **9% Daily Value**
Monounsaturated Fat **1g**	Calcium **19% Daily Value**
Trans Fat **3g**	Iron **17% Daily Value**
Cholesterol **46mg**	

Zucchini, Pesto & Sausage Pizza

Makes: 3

You can make these vegetable pizzas even more colorful by substituting a yellow squash or yellow pepper for half the zucchini. Lose the crushed red pepper if your kids don't like the heat. Cut the zucchini and mozzarella into thin slices to ensure tender squash and expertly melted cheese in less than 10 minutes.

INGREDIENTS

3 oz. mild Italian ground turkey sausage

1 cup thinly sliced zucchini

¼ cup basil pesto, divided

1 (12-oz.) package of 3 (7-inch) prebaked pizza crusts

3 oz. fresh mozzarella cheese, very thinly sliced

⅛ tsp. crushed red pepper

2 tbsp. fresh basil leaves

INSTRUCTIONS

1. Preheat the oven to 450°F.

2. Heat a small nonstick skillet over medium-high heat. Add the sausage and cook, stirring and breaking up the sausage with a wooden spoon, until cooked through, 4 to 5 minutes. Transfer the sausage to a plate. Add the zucchini and 1 tablespoon of the pesto to the skillet. Cook, stirring often, until the zucchini is slightly tender, about 3 minutes. Remove from the heat.

3. Place the pizza crusts on a baking sheet and spread the remaining 3 tablespoons of pesto evenly over the crusts. Top each crust evenly with the zucchini mixture, sausage, mozzarella cheese and red pepper. Bake until the crusts are crisped on the edges and the cheese is melted, 7 to 8 minutes. Remove from the oven, and sprinkle evenly with the basil. Cut each pizza into 4 slices and serve immediately.

NUTRITION DATA FOR 1 SERVING:

Calories **392kcal**	Sodium **782mg**
Total Carbohydrates **44g**	Potassium **576mg**
Protein **15g**	Dietary Fiber **6g**
Total Fat **22g**	Sugars **4g**
Saturated Fat **6g**	Vitamin A **10% Daily Value**
Polyunsaturated Fat **8g**	Vitamin C **8% Daily Value**
Monounsaturated Fat **6g**	Calcium **21% Daily Value**
Trans Fat **2g**	Iron **19% Daily Value**
Cholesterol **60mg**	

Chicken & Cucumber Salad with Parsley Pesto

Serves: 6

This hearty salad is a lean protein powerhouse, thanks to chicken, chickpeas and edamame. The parsley pesto provides vitamin K to strengthen bones. Choose frozen shelled edamame to make this meal faster.

INGREDIENTS

2 cups packed, fresh flat-leaf parsley leaves (from 1 bunch)

1 cup fresh baby spinach

2 tbsp. fresh lemon juice

1 tbsp. grated Parmesan cheese

1 tsp. toasted pine nuts

1 medium clove garlic, smashed

1 tsp. kosher salt

¼ tsp. black pepper

½ cup extra virgin olive oil

4 cups shredded rotisserie chicken (from 1 chicken)

2 cups cooked and shelled edamame

1 (15-oz.) can unsalted chickpeas, drained and rinsed

1 cup chopped English cucumber

4 cups loosely packed arugula

INSTRUCTIONS

1. Combine the parsley, spinach, lemon juice, cheese, pine nuts, garlic, salt and pepper in the bowl of a food processor; process until smooth, about 1 minute. With the processor running, add the oil and process until smooth, about 1 minute longer.

2. Stir together the chicken, edamame, chickpeas and cucumber in a large bowl. Add the pesto and toss to combine.

3. Place ⅔ cup arugula in each of 6 bowls; top each with 1 cup of the chicken salad mixture. Serve immediately.

NUTRITION DATA FOR 1 SERVING:

Calories **482kcal**	Sodium **465mg**
Total Carbohydrates **22g**	Potassium **345mg**
Protein **40g**	Dietary Fiber **7g**
Total Fat **26g**	Sugars **2g**
Saturated Fat **4g**	Vitamin A **6% Daily Value**
Polyunsaturated Fat **15g**	Vitamin C **12% Daily Value**
Monounsaturated Fat **4g**	Calcium **17% Daily Value**
Trans Fat **3g**	Iron **21% Daily Value**
Cholesterol **46mg**	

Serves: 5

Here's a short version of Spain's favorite romesco sauce. It has so many smoky flavors!

Gnocchi with Spinach and Pepper Sauce

INGREDIENTS

16 oz. whole-wheat potato gnocchi

5 oz. baby spinach

1½ oz. Manchego cheese, grated (about ¼ cup plus 2 tbsp.), divided

3 tbsp. olive oil, divided

½ cup chopped jarred roasted red peppers

¼ cup smoked almonds

1 plum tomato, chopped

1 slice baguette, torn (about ½ oz.)

1 clove garlic

½ tsp. paprika

¼ tsp. crushed red pepper

2 tbsp. sherry vinegar

INSTRUCTIONS

1. Cook the gnocchi according to the package directions, but do not salt the cooking water. Drain and return the gnocchi to the pot. Over medium heat add the spinach, ¼ cup of the cheese and 1 tablespoon of the olive oil. Cover and let stand until the spinach wilts, 2 to 3 minutes. Gently toss to combine evenly.

2. In a food processor, combine the red peppers, almonds, tomato, baguette, garlic, paprika, crushed red pepper, vinegar and remaining 2 tablespoons olive oil and pulse until smooth, about 1 minute.

3. Divide the gnocchi mixture among 5 bowls. Top evenly with the sauce and sprinkle with the remaining 2 tablespoons cheese.

NUTRITION DATA FOR 1 SERVING:

Calories **324kcal**
Total Carbohydrates **34g**
Protein **9g**
Total Fat **16g**
Saturated Fat **4g**
Polyunsaturated Fat **7g**
Monounsaturated Fat **3g**
Trans Fat **2g**
Cholesterol **56mg**
Sodium **590mg**
Potassium **325mg**
Dietary Fiber **8g**
Sugars **2g**
Vitamin A **8% Daily Value**
Vitamin C **12% Daily Value**
Calcium **14% Daily Value**
Iron **7% Daily Value**

Serves: 4

As a quick-cooking whole grain, bulgur is perfect for time-crunched weeknight cooking. If you can't find it in the grains section, you can replace it with quinoa or whole-wheat couscous.

Chicken & Bulgur Salad with Peaches

INGREDIENTS

1⅓ cups water

⅔ cup bulgur

1 lb. chicken breast cutlets

1 tsp. kosher salt, divided

½ tsp. black pepper

4 cups packed arugula

2 cups halved cherry tomatoes

2 cups sliced fresh peaches

3 tbsp. extra-virgin olive oil

2 tbsp. rice vinegar

INSTRUCTIONS

1. Combine the water and bulgur in a small saucepan over medium heat and bring to a boil. Lower the heat to medium-low, cover and simmer for 10 minutes. Drain, rinse the bulgur under cold water, then drain again and spread out on paper towels to dry.

2. Meanwhile, coat a grill pan with cooking spray and place over high heat. Sprinkle the chicken with ½ teaspoon of both the salt and the pepper. Transfer to the hot pan and grill, turning occasionally, until done, 6 to 7 minutes. Remove to a cutting board and let stand for 3 minutes, then slice against the grain into strips.

3. Place the bulgur, arugula, tomatoes and peaches in a large bowl. Add the remaining ½ teaspoon salt and the oil and vinegar; toss to coat. Divide the mixture among 4 plates and top evenly with the chicken.

NUTRITION DATA FOR 1 SERVING:

Calories **364kcal**	Sodium **547mg**
Total Carbohydrates **30g**	Potassium **475mg**
Protein **31g**	Dietary Fiber **6g**
Total Fat **14g**	Sugars **9g**
Saturated Fat **2g**	Vitamin A **5% Daily Value**
Polyunsaturated Fat **6g**	Vitamin C **9% Daily Value**
Monounsaturated Fat **4g**	Calcium **7% Daily Value**
Trans Fat **2g**	Iron **20% Daily Value**
Cholesterol **47mg**	

Almond-Crusted Trout with Swiss Chard

Serves: 4

Baking with almost flour gives fish a nice crisp texture without using much oil. An added plus: almond flour is gluten-free, and a light coating of mustard will help it adhere to the trout fillets.

All you need is a splash of white wine to add a hit of acidity to balance the garlicky greens.

INGREDIENTS

1⅓ oz. almond flour (about ½ cup)

4 (4-5-oz.) trout fillets, skin on

1 tbsp. Dijon mustard

2½ tbsp. grapeseed oil or canola oil, divided

½ tsp. kosher salt, divided

½ tsp. black pepper, divided

4 cups thinly sliced Swiss chard leaves and stems (about 5 oz.), divided

3 cloves garlic, thinly sliced

¼ cup dry white wine

1 tbsp. fresh lemon juice

1 tbsp. unsalted butter

1 tbsp. minced fresh chives

4 lemon wedges

INSTRUCTIONS

1. Place the almond flour in a shallow bowl. Brush the flesh side of each fish fillet with mustard, then gently press the mustard side of each fillet into the almond flour, leaving the skin side bare. Heat 1 tablespoon of the oil in a large nonstick skillet over medium-high heat. Add 2 fillets, flesh side down, and cook until golden brown and lightly crispy, 2 to 3 minutes.

2. Flip the fillets and cook until the flesh is flaky and the fish is cooked through, about 4–6 minutes. Transfer to a paper towel–lined plate. Wipe the skillet clean, then repeat with another tablespoon of oil and the remaining 2 fillets. Sprinkle the cooked fillets evenly with ¼ teaspoon of the salt and ¼ teaspoon of the pepper.

3. Wipe the skillet clean. Add the remaining 1½ teaspoons oil to the skillet and heat over medium-high heat. Add the chard and cook, stirring occasionally, until slightly tender, 3 to 4 minutes. Add the garlic and cook, stirring often, until fragrant, about 1 minute. Add the wine and lemon juice and cook until slightly reduced, about 1 minute. Stir in the butter and season with the remaining

4. ¼ teaspoon salt and ¼ teaspoon pepper. Divide the chard mixture among 4 plates. Top each with a fish fillet and sprinkle evenly with chives. Serve each plate with a lemon wedge on the side.

NUTRITION DATA FOR 1 SERVING:

Calories **368kcal**	Sodium **591mg**
Total Carbohydrates **6g**	Potassium **478mg**
Protein **27g**	Dietary Fiber **2g**
Total Fat **25g**	Sugars **1g**
Saturated Fat **5g**	Vitamin A **8% Daily Value**
Polyunsaturated Fat **8g**	Vitamin C **10% Daily Value**
Monounsaturated Fat **6g**	Calcium **17% Daily Value**
Trans Fat **5g**	Iron **9% Daily Value**
Cholesterol **72mg**	

Saffron Fish Stew with White Beans

Serves: 4

Succulent pieces of white fish go perfectly in saffron soup with beans and sliced tomatoes. This is a quick, easy and satisfying soup that can be prepared in half an hour, making it perfect for a busy week.

INGREDIENTS

- 1 tbsp. extra-virgin olive oil
- 1 cup chopped onion
- 2 garlic cloves, crushed
- 1 sprig thyme
- 1 tsp. ground fennel
- ½ tsp. ground coriander
- ½ tsp. fresh orange peel
- ¼ tsp. saffron threads
- 1½ cups water
- 1½ cups clam juice
- 1 (14.5-oz.) can diced tomatoes with liquid
- 1 lb. flounder fillet, cut into 2-inch pieces
- 1 (14-oz.) can Great Northern beans, rinsed and drained
- ⅛ tsp. salt
- fresh thyme, about 5 leaves

INSTRUCTIONS

1. Heat the oil in a large Dutch oven over medium-high heat. Add the onion, garlic, thyme, fennel and coriander and sauté for 5 minutes. Stir in the orange peel and saffron, then add the water, clam juice and tomatoes.

2. Bring to a boil, then reduce the heat and simmer for 5 minutes. Stir in the fish, beans and salt and cook for 5 minutes more. Divide the stew among 4 bowls and serve topped with the thyme leaves.

NUTRITION DATA FOR 1 SERVING:

Calories **249kcal**	Sodium **495mg**
Total Carbohydrates **23g**	Potassium **296mg**
Protein **28g**	Dietary Fiber **7g**
Total Fat **5g**	Sugars **1g**
Saturated Fat **3g**	Vitamin A **6% Daily Value**
Polyunsaturated Fat **1g**	Vitamin C **9% Daily Value**
Monounsaturated Fat **2g**	Calcium **15% Daily Value**
Trans Fat **1g**	Iron **22% Daily Value**
Cholesterol **46mg**	

Beef Kofta Patties with Cucumber Salad

Serves: 4

These beef kofta cakes with cucumber salad are full of flavor. Prepare to transport your taste buds to a beach in Spain on a nice summer day!. A little vacation without ever leaving the kitchen table—what's not to love about these kofta patties?

INGREDIENTS

1 lb. ground sirloin

¼ cup plus 2 tbsp. chopped, fresh flat-leaf parsley, divided

¼ cup chopped fresh cilantro

1 tbsp. chopped fresh ginger

2 tsp. ground coriander

1 tsp. ground cumin

½ tsp. ground cinnamon

½ tsp. salt

2 cups thinly sliced English cucumber

2 tbsp. rice vinegar

½ cup plain, fat-free Greek yogurt

1 tbsp. fresh lemon juice

½ tsp. freshly ground black pepper

2 (6-inch) pitas, quartered

INSTRUCTIONS

1. Heat a grill pan over medium-high heat. Combine the beef, ¼ cup of the parsley, the cilantro, ginger, coriander, cumin, cinnamon and salt in a medium bowl.

2. Divide the beef mixture into 4 equal portions and shape each into a ½-inch-thick patty. Place the patties in the pan and cook for 3 minutes on each side, or to your desired degree of doneness.

3. Meanwhile, in a medium bowl, combine the cucumber and vinegar and toss well. In a small bowl, combine the yogurt, the remaining 2 tablespoons parsley, and the lemon juice and pepper; stir with a whisk. Arrange 1 patty and ½ cup cucumber mixture on each of 4 plates. Top each serving with about 2 tablespoons of the yogurt sauce. Serve each with 2 pita wedges.

NUTRITION DATA FOR 1 SERVING:

Calories **321kcal**	Sodium **518mg**
Total Carbohydrates **22g**	Potassium **420mg**
Protein **29g**	Dietary Fiber **4g**
Total Fat **12g**	Sugars **4g**
Saturated Fat **5g**	Vitamin A **4% Daily Value**
Polyunsaturated Fat **1g**	Vitamin C **11% Daily Value**
Monounsaturated Fat **3g**	Calcium **25% Daily Value**
Trans Fat **2g**	Iron **14% Daily Value**
Cholesterol **64mg**	

Halibut with Lemon-Fennel Salad

Serves: 4

Fennel is a delicate, sweet-flavored, licorice-scented vegetable. It contains anethole and cineole, which have an antibacterial effect that can help with indigestion-related issues. These compounds also have an expectorant effect, helping to clear the lungs.

INGREDIENTS

1 tsp. ground coriander

½ tsp. ground cumin

½ tsp. salt

¼ tsp. freshly ground black pepper

5 tsp. extra virgin olive oil, divided

2 cloves garlic, minced

4 (6-oz.) halibut fillets

2 cups thinly sliced fennel bulb

¼ cup thinly sliced red onion

2 tbsp. fresh lemon juice

1 tbsp. chopped fresh flat-leaf parsley

1 tsp. fresh thyme leaves

INSTRUCTIONS

1. In a small bowl, combine the coriander, cumin, salt and pepper. In a separate small bowl, combine 1½ teaspoons of the spice mixture with 2 teaspoons of the oil and the garlic; rub this garlic mixture evenly over the fish.

2. Heat 1 teaspoon of oil in a large nonstick skillet over medium-high heat. Add the fish and cook for 5 minutes on each side, or to your desired degree of doneness.

3. Meanwhile, combine the remaining ⅓ teaspoon spice mixture and the remaining 2 teaspoons oil with the fennel, onion, lemon juice, parsley and thyme in a medium bowl, tossing well to coat. Serve the salad alongside the fish.

NUTRITION DATA FOR 1 SERVING:

Calories **259kcal**
Total Carbohydrates **5g**
Protein **36.3g**
Total Fat **10g**
Saturated Fat **1g**
Polyunsaturated Fat **3g**
Monounsaturated Fat **4g**
Trans Fat **2g**
Cholesterol **54mg**
Sodium **780mg**
Potassium **356mg**
Dietary Fiber **5g**
Sugars **2g**
Vitamin A **6% Daily Value**
Vitamin C **15% Daily Value**
Calcium **35% Daily Value**
Iron **16% Daily Value**

Caprese Chicken

Serves: 4

This is a pretty straightforward recipe with basic ingredients. It's destined to become your favorite summertime dinner. The chicken is prepared with olive oil, salt, pepper and Italian seasoning. If you don't have Italian seasoning, just substitute equal parts garlic powder, dried basil and dried oregano instead.

INGREDIENTS

2 tbsp. olive oil, divided

2 lb. boneless, skinless chicken breasts

1 tsp. salt

1 tsp. black pepper

1 tsp. chili powder

1 tbsp. dried Italian seasoning

1 tsp. sweet paprika

8 thick slices ripe tomato

8 (1-oz.) slices fresh mozzarella cheese

8 medium basil leaves

4 tbsp. balsamic glaze or balsamic reduction

INSTRUCTIONS

1. Preheat the oven to 350°F.

2. Heat large cast iron pan over medium heat and add 1 tablespoon of the olive oil.

3. While your oil is heating up, butterfly the chicken: cut each chicken breast from the side about three-quarters of the way through, then open the chicken and lay flat.

4. Season each chicken breast with the remaining 1 tablespoon of olive oil, salt, pepper, chili powder, Italian seasoning and sweet paprika.

5. Place 2 slices of tomato, 2 slices of mozzarella cheese and 2 basil leaves on one side of each chicken breast. Close the chicken breasts and use toothpicks to help keep them closed around the filling.

6. Transfer the stuffed chicken breasts to the pan and sear for about 5 minutes on each side, until golden brown.

7. Transfer to the oven until the internal tempurature reaches 165°F.

8. Transfer the chicken breasts to a plate and let rest 3–5 minutes.

9. Slice into ¼-inch slices and drizzle the balsamic glaze over the top of the chicken. Serve over your favorite salad: we suggest the Rustic Avocodo and Corn Salad on page 150.

NUTRITION DATA FOR 1 SERVING:

Calories **366kcal**	Sodium **387mg**
Total Carbohydrates **4g**	Potassium **23mg**
Protein **35g**	Dietary Fiber **1g**
Total Fat **12g**	Sugars **2g**
Saturated Fat **5g**	Vitamin A **35 % Daily Value**
Polyunsaturated fat **3g**	Vitamin C **15 % Daily Value**
Monounsaturated fat **5g**	Calcium **15 % Daily Value**
Trans fat **0g**	Iron **10% Daily Value**
Cholesterol **85mg**	

Rustic Avocado & Corn Salad

Serves: 2

Here's the perfect light meal for lunch that you can easily customize to your own taste and preferences. High in calcium and fiber, it can be made in a matter of minutes and served with either your favorite chicken or fish.

INGREDIENTS

2 avocados, diced

2 medium red onions, diced

2 cups cherry tomatoes

2 cups sweet corn

1 cup feta cheese

2 tbsp. finely chopped fresh cilantro

2 tbsp. finely chopped fresh parsley

2 tbsp. Italian dressing

1 lime, juiced

salt, to taste

pepper, to taste

INSTRUCTIONS

1. Arrange the avocado, onion, tomatoes, corn, and feta cheese in 2 medium bowls, giving each ingredient its own section and filling in all the gaps.

2. Sprinkle the cilantro and parsley over the top. Drizzle the dressing and the lime juice over the salad, then season with salt and pepper, to taste.

3. Serve with grilled chicken or salmon, or with our own favorite, the Chicken Caprese on page 148.

NUTRITION DATA FOR 1 SERVING:

Calories **422kcal**	Sodium **298mg**
Total Carbohydrates **18g**	Potassium **17mg**
Protein **40g**	Dietary Fiber **21g**
Total Fat **29g**	Sugars **9g**
Saturated Fat **8g**	Vitamin A **45%**
Polyunsaturated fat **18g**	Vitamin C **23%**
Monounsaturated fat **9g**	Calcium **28%**
Trans fat **4g**	Iron **22%**
Cholesterol **45mg**	

Chicken Piccata

Serves: 6

This Chicken Piccata is going to be your new favorite chicken dish for sure! Garlic, lemon, butter and chicken—flavor combinations don't get much better than this. The juicy chicken breasts are served with a generous amount of the sauce poured over the top. The addition of capers brings an extra zing that we think makes this dish absolutely perfect. Serve alongside your preferred seasonal salad or lightly steamed Mediterranean vegetables for a well-balanced meal.

INGREDIENTS

2 lbs. (3 large) boneless, skinless chicken breasts

1 tbsp. black pepper

⅓ cup flour

¼ cup olive oil

5 cloves garlic, sliced

¼ cup white wine

¼ cup demi-glace (optional)

1 lemon, juiced

6 lemon slices

½ cup butter

2 tbsp. finely chopped parsley, plus more for garnish

1 tsp. capers

INSTRUCTIONS

1. Slice each chicken breast in half horizontally to make 6 fillets altogether. Gently pound the meat with a mallet until each fillet is thin and flat but not broken. Sprinkle the meat with the black pepper and dredge lightly in the flour.

2. Preheat a wide, heavy skillet over medium heat. Add the olive oil and garlic and sauté until lightly browned, then remove the garlic with a slotted spoon and set aside.

3. Turn the heat up to high and add the chicken. Cook 2–3 minutes per side until golden brown.

4. Remove the chicken to a serving platter and set aside.

5. Drain the oil from the pan, then return the pan to the heat and add the white wine. Cook, stirring, to deglaze the pan for about 1 minute. Add the demi-glace, if using, the lemon juice and the reserved garlic.

6. Stir well to heat the sauce thoroughly, then add the butter and stir until fully melted and combined. At this point, you can remove the garlic with a slotted spoon or leave in.

7. Stir in the parsley, then spoon the sauce over the chicken.

8. Garnish with the capers, lemon slices, and more freshly chopped parsley.

NUTRITION DATA FOR 1 SERVING:

Calories **463kcal**
Total Carbohydrates **7g**
Protein **37g**
Total Fat **32g**
Saturated Fat **14g**
Polyunsaturated Fat **2g**
Monounsaturated Fat **15g**
Trans Fat **0g**
Cholesterol **170mg**
Sodium **407mg**
Potassium **38mg**
Dietary Fiber **0.4g**
Sugars **0.2g**
Vitamin A **12% Daily Value**
Vitamin C **6% Daily Value**
Calcium **1% Daily Value**
Iron **2% Daily Value**

Serves: 6

This is an excellent recipe for when you are entertaining. There is something so amazing about getting together around a table of food with loved ones for a meal. This recipe is also extremely versatile—feel free to use any mixture of leafy greens you like, such as arugula or spinach leaves, and to add in sliced cucumber or bell peppers. Even some grilled eggplant would go wonderfully. This is a lovely way to incorporate lots of fresh, local, seasonal produce into your meal.

Falafel Tortillas with Tahini Sauce

INGREDIENTS

FOR THE FALAFEL:

1 (24-oz.) can chickpeas, drained and rinsed

1 medium onion, grated

4 scallions, minced

1 bunch parsley, finely chopped

2 tbsp. chopped fresh cilantro

1 tsp. garlic, chopped

2 tsp. ground corinader

2 tsp. ground cumin

½ tsp. baking powder

2–3 cups canola oil, for deep frying

INSTRUCTIONS

1. To make the batter, remove the skins from the chickpeas by rubbing them with a dish towel.

2. Place the skinned chickpeas in the bowl of a food processor and purée. Add the onions, scallions, parsley, cilantro, garlic, coriander, cumin and baking powder. Blend the ingredients together until a smooth paste forms (add a little water if necessary).

3. Let the mixture rest for 30 minutes.

4. Meanwhile, make the tahini sauce. In a small bowl combine the tahini, water and lemon juice. Mix together to form a smooth sauce, adding more water if necessary.

5. Add the garlic, parsley and black pepper and mix until well blended. Set the sauce aside.

6. To fry the falafel, fill a medium to large saucepan or pot with enough oil for deep frying about ¼ inch, and place over medium-high heat.

recipe continues

FOR THE TAHINI SAUCE:

⅔ cup tahini (sesame paste)

3 tbsp. tater, plus more as needed

2 lemons, juiced

2 cloves garlic, minced

2 tbsp. minced fresh parsley

1 tsp. black pepper

TO SERVE:

6 medium/large tortillas or pita breads, warmed

1 ½ cups mixed lettuce leaves

1 ½ cups halved cherry tomatoes

6 lemon wedges

7. When the oil is hot, use a small, 1 oz. (½-inch) ice cream scoop to scoop the falafel mixture into balls and drop each one into the hot oil, working in batches if necessary. Deep-fry each batch for 2 to 3 minutes, or until the falafel are golden brown.

8. Remove from the oil with a slotted spoon and set on a paper towel–lined plate to drain. Repeat to fry the remaining batter.

9. To serve, set the falafel, tahini sauce, and other fixings on the table and allow your guests to assemble their own tortillas. Lay a tortilla down and add a bed of lettuce, then top with cherry tomatoes and falafel. Squeeze over some lemon juice and top with the tahini sauce, fold and enjoy.

NUTRITION DATA FOR 1 SERVING:

Calories **668kcal**	Sodium **707mg**
Total Carbohydrates **61g**	Potassium **466mg**
Protein **16g**	Dietary Fiber **12g**
Total Fat **42g**	Sugars **3g**
Saturated Fat **6g**	Vitamin A **20% Daily Value**
Polyunsaturated Fat **13g**	Vitamin C **38% Daily Value**
Monounsaturated Fat **8g**	Calcium **18% Daily Value**
Trans Fat **0g**	Iron **31% Daily Value**
Cholesterol **0mg**	

Italian Meatball Wedding Soup

Serves: 8

I get really excited whenever I make Italian wedding soup. It's one of my favorite dishes, filled with homemade browned meatballs, fresh veggies and tiny bits of pasta. It's perfect for any time of the day and never disappoints!

INGREDIENTS

FOR THE MEATBALLS:

1 large egg

3 tbsp. finely chopped fresh chives

2 tsp. finely chopped fresh sage

2 cloves garlic, minced

⅓ lb. 85% or 90% lean ground beef

½ lb. sweet or hot Italian sausage, removed from the casings

½ cup grated Parmigiano-Reggiano

⅓ cup Italian-seasoned bread crumbs

¼ tsp. salt

FOR THE SOUP:

2 tbsp. olive oil

1 medium yellow onion, diced

INSTRUCTIONS

1. Preheat the oven to 350°F. Line a baking sheet with aluminum foil, then set an ovenproof roasting rack on top. Generously spray the rack with nonstick cooking spray.

2. In a medium bowl, beat the egg together with the chives, sage and garlic. Add all the remaining meatball ingredients and mash with your hands until well combined. Roll the mixture into tablespoon-size balls (about 1 inch in diameter each) and place on the prepared rack. Bake until lightly browned and cooked through, about 18 minutes.

3. Meanwhile, heat the olive oil in a medium soup pot until shimmering. Add the onions, carrots and celery and cook, stirring frequently, until the vegetables are well softened, about 8 minutes. Add the chicken broth, beef broth, water, wine, if using, bay leaf, salt and pepper and bring to a boil for about 8 minutes.

4. Cook the pasta according to the package directions until al dente, about 7 minutes. Taste the soup and adjust the seasoning if necessary, then lower the heat and add the spinach and meatballs. Simmer for a few minutes, until the

recipe continues

- 2 large carrots, diced
- 2 stalks celery, diced
- 6 cups high-quality chicken broth, such as Swanson (do not use low-sodium)
- 2 cups high-quality beef broth, such as Swanson (do not use low-sodium)
- 2 cups water
- ½ cup dry white wine (optional)
- 1 bay leaf
- ½ tsp. salt
- ¼ tsp. white pepper (or black pepper)
- 1 cup small pasta, such as ditalini
- 4 oz. fresh spinach, stems trimmed, roughly chopped (about 3 packed cups)
- Parmesan cheese for serving

spinach is wilted and the meatballs are warmed all the way through. Transfer the soup to bowls and serve with the grated Parmesan cheese.

NUTRITION DATA FOR 1 SERVING:

Calories **359kcal**	Sodium **930mg**
Total Carbohydrates **16g**	Potassium **21mg**
Protein **23g**	Dietary Fiber **2g**
Total Fat **22g**	Sugars **5g**
Saturated fat **7g**	Vitamin A **10%**
Polyunsaturated fat **0.5g**	Vitamin C **0%**
Monounsaturated fat **2g**	Calcium **4%**
Trans fat **3g**	Iron **3**
Cholesterol **83mg**	

Fish in Island Sauce

Serves: 6

Simple, light and healthy dishes can at times create the most comforting and satisfying meals. This recipe is versatile—we suggest grouper, but any white-fleshed fish will taste just as good—so pick one that you prefer, and try to choose whatever is fresh and local.

This delicate, delicious dish can be served up within 20 minutes of opening the refrigerator door, and its perfect balance of flavors, including pops of tanginess from the capers, will leave you hankering for more.

INGREDIENTS

3 tbsp. olive oil

6 cloves garlic, minced

6 grouper or other white-fleshed fish fillets (3 lbs.)

2 onions, peeled and diced

1 can (15 oz.) diced tomatoes, drained

1 green bell pepper, seeded and diced

½ cup drained capers

2 tbsp. finely chopped parsley

2 tbsp. white wine vinegar

1 bay leaf

INSTRUCTIONS

1. Heat the oil in a large skillet over medium-high heat. Add the garlic and cook until golden, about 2 minutes.

2. Add the fish fillets and cook, turning once, until golden and cooked through and the fish flakes easily with a fork, approximately 3 minutes on each side.

3. Remove the fish from the skillet, cover to keep warm and set aside.

4. Add the onion to the skillet and sauté until transparent, about 5 minutes.

5. Mix the tomatoes and bell pepper and continue to sauté for another 5 to 6 minutes.

6. Add the capers, parsley, vinegar and bay leaf. Bring to a boil and cook for another 10 minutes.

7. Place a fish fillet on each plate, pour the sauce over the fish and serve immediately.

NUTRITION DATA FOR 1 SERVING:

Calories **223kcal**
Total Carbohydrates **10g**
Protein **26g**
Total Fat **9g**
Saturated Fat **1g**
Polyunsaturated Fat **1g**
Monounsaturated Fat **5g**
Trans Fat **0.4g**
Cholesterol **61mg**
Sodium **696mg**
Potassium **235mg**
Dietary Fiber **2g**
Sugars **4g**
Vitamin A **16% Daily Value**
Vitamin C **55% Daily Value**
Calcium **7% Daily Value**
Iron **13% Daily Value**

Serves: 6

Shellfish is not only an important and popular part of a Mediterranean diet, it is also a pivotal part of a nutritionally dense diet. You can use any type of small clams, cockles or mussels for this recipe. Select local live shellfish where possible for superior taste and freshness.

When cooking shellfish, be sure not to overdo it, as shellfish can become quite rubbery if cooked for too long. If you are unable to get a hold of fregola to use for this recipe, Israeli couscous will be a great substitute.

Fregola with Clams and Chilis

INGREDIENTS

1 lb. fregola

¼ cup olive oil

1 medium red onion, peeled and thinly sliced

4 cloves garlic, peeled and thinly sliced

2 oz. prosciutto, diced into ⅛-inch pieces

1 lb. tiny clams (such as Manilas), cockles or mussels, scrubbed and rinsed

1 cup dry white wine

1 cup chicken stock

½ cup tomato puree

1 pinch saffron

1 tbsp. crushed red pepper

salt and black pepper

1 bunch Italian parsley, leaves only

INSTRUCTIONS

1. Cook the fregola according to the package instructions until just cooked, approximately 15 minutes.

2. Meanwhile, in a medium saucepan, heat the olive oil to smoking over medium-high heat.

3. Add the onion, garlic and prosciutto and sauté until softened, about 5–8 minutes.

4. Add the clams, white wine, chicken stock, tomato purée and saffron and bring to a boil. Cover and cook 5–8 minutes, until most of the clams have opened. Discard any that haven't opened.

5. Add the cooked fregola to the clams and cook 3-5 minutes longer until the texture resembles risotto.

6. Add the crushed red pepper and stir to combine.

7. Season with salt and black pepper, to taste, garnish with a generous amount of parsley and serve immediately.

NUTRITION DATA FOR 1 SERVING:

Calories **511kcal**	Monounsaturated Fat **8g**	Sugars **4g**
Total Carbohydrates **68g**	Trans Fat **0.2g**	Vitamin A **16% Daily Value**
Protein **23g**	Cholesterol **31mg**	Vitamin C **31% Daily Value**
Total Fat **13g**	Sodium **451mg**	Calcium **3% Daily Value**
Saturated Fat **2g**	Potassium **584mg**	Iron **69% Daily Value**
Polyunsaturated Fat **2g**	Dietary Fiber **5g**	

Meat Loaf Stuffed with Prosciutto & Cheese

Serves: 6

Meat loaf must be one of the best comfort foods around! We have created a Mediterranean-inspired dish stuffed full of prosciutto and creamy mozzarella. This meat loaf requires a tiny bit more effort than a regular one—however, that little extra effort will be so worth it!

As soon as you take a bite and get some of that creamy melted mozzarella, paired perfectly with the prosciutto and the flavors of Mediterranean vegetables and herbs, we guarantee you won't be trying another meat loaf recipe anytime soon.

INGREDIENTS

FOR THE MEAT LOAF:

1¼ lb. ground beef

1 large onion, finely chopped

1 green bell pepper, seeded and finely chopped

1 cup bread crumbs, plus more as needed

2 tbsp. chopped fresh parsley

1 clove garlic, minced

1 (10.75-oz.) can tomato soup

2 large eggs, lightly beaten

1 tsp. prepared mustard, preferably Dijon

½ tsp. dried oregano

⅛ tsp. salt

⅛ tsp. black pepper

FOR THE STUFFING:

6–8 slices prosciutto

1 cup shredded mozzarella cheese

INSTRUCTIONS

1. Preheat the oven to 375°F. Lightly oil a 9 by 5-inch pan.
2. In a large bowl, combine all the meat loaf ingredients and mix with your hands until well combined. Add more bread crumbs if necessary, one tablespoon at a time, until the mixture is firm enough to shape into a loaf.
3. Lightly spray a large piece of aluminium foil or nonstick baking paper. Turn the meat mixture out onto the foil and form it into a 12 by 8-inch rectangle.
4. Arrange the prosciutto on top of the meat, leaving a small margin around the edges. Sprinkle the shredded mozzarella cheese on top of the prosciutto slices.
5. Starting from the short end, carefully roll the meat mixture jelly-roll style. Seal the edges and ends by pressing and pinch the meat loaf together at the ends and along the seam. Place the loaf seam side up in the prepared pan.
6. Bake for 1 hour or until it reaches an internal temperature of 165°F.
7. Serve with your choice of steamed vegetables or side salad.

NUTRITION DATA FOR 1 SERVING:

Calories **446kcal**	Sodium **990mg**
Total Carbohydrates **28g**	Potassium **758mg**
Protein **32g**	Dietary Fiber **3g**
Total Fat **22g**	Sugars **8g**
Saturated Fat **9g**	Vitamin A **20% Daily Value**
Polyunsaturated Fat **1g**	Vitamin C **62% Daily Value**
Monounsaturated Fat **8g**	Calcium **20% Daily Value**
Trans Fat **1g**	Iron **25% Daily Value**
Cholesterol **153mg**	

Serves: 6

When you think of Mediterranean meals, classics such as spaghetti and meatballs may come to mind. We have emphasized the Mediterranean flavors in these meatballs with a wonderfully delicious yet easy sauce.

This dish is full of classic Mediterranean vegetables such as eggplant, zucchini, bell peppers and tomatoes, giving it a power punch in the nutritional department as well as a rich, strong flavor. You can guarantee that serving this simple, enjoyable pasta dish at your dinner table will have even the fussiest eaters coming back for more.

Mediterranean Meatballs

INGREDIENTS

FOR THE SAUCE:

3 tbsp. olive oil

2 cloves garlic, minced

2 onions, peeled and diced

2 green peppers, seeded and diced

2 zucchini, diced

1 large eggplant, peeled and cubed

4 tomatoes, peeled and chopped

¼ cup freshly chopped parsley

½ tsp. dried thyme

½ cup chicken stock

salt and black pepper, to taste

INSTRUCTIONS

1. To make the sauce, heat the olive oil in a large skillet or saucepan over medium-high heat. Add the garlic and sauté until the garlic starts to brown.

2. Add the onion and continue to sauté until translucent.

3. Add the green peppers, zucchini, eggplant and tomatoes. Continue to cook for 7 minutes, then add the parsley, thyme, chicken stock and salt and pepper, to taste. Reduce the heat and allow to simmer, uncovered, for approximately 40 minutes to make a thick sauce.

4. Meanwhile, make the meatballs. Place the bread in the bowl of a food processor and pulse a few times until it resembles crumbs; set aside.

5. In a large bowl mix the ground meat with the Parmesan cheese, nutmeg, salt and pepper.

6. Roll the meat mixture into balls about 1 inch wide. Dip each ball into the beaten egg and then into the bread crumbs; set the coated balls aside.

FOR THE MEATBALLS:

2 slices white or whole-wheat bread

1½ lb. ground beef

⅓ cup Parmesan cheese

¼ tsp. nutmeg

2 tsp. salt

2 tsp. black pepper

1 egg, lightly beaten

2–4 tbsp. olive oil

TO SERVE:

1 cup cooked spaghetti (or other pasta of choice)

Parmesan cheese

chopped fresh parsley

7. Heat the olive oil in a large skillet over medium-high heat. Add the meatballs and fry on each side 6–8 minutes until golden brown. Remove the cooked meatballs from the pan, drop into the sauce, and gently stir.

8. Serve the meatballs and sauce over the cooked spaghetti. Sprinkle with more Parmesan cheese if desired, and garnish with fresh parsley.

NUTRITION DATA FOR 1 SERVING:

Calories **555kcal**	Sodium **328mg**
Total Carbohydrates **43g**	Potassium **1072mg**
Protein **33g**	Dietary Fiber **7g**
Total Fat **28g**	Sugars **8g**
Saturated Fat **9g**	Vitamin A **25% Daily Value**
Polyunsaturated Fat **2g**	Vitamin C **94% Daily Value**
Monounsaturated Fat **14g**	Calcium **17% Daily Value**
Trans Fat **1g**	Iron **26% Daily Value**
Cholesterol **115mg**	

Neapolitan Polenta Pie

Serves: 4

This hearty and flavorful Neapolitan Polenta Pie is a great way to serve polenta a little differently. It will quite possibly become your *favorite* way.

There is a little time involved in making the "cheese" for this recipe; however, if time does not allow, you may be able to find some delicious, creamy, ready-made labneh from most good delis. Once you have the "cheese" ready to go, this meal comes together very easily. This is definitely comfort food at its finest, hearty and loaded with the traditional flavors we all love. We guarantee this meatless Mediterranean dish will become a firm family favorite.

INGREDIENTS

12 oz. plain Greek yogurt

1 tsp. sea salt, divided

3 cups water

1 cup polenta

1½ cups pizza sauce

1 cup thinly sliced red onion

1 tomato, sliced

1 cup sliced green bell pepper

¼ lb. wild mushrooms, washed and sliced

2 oz. dried porcini mushrooms, soaked and drained.

3 tbsp. capers

⅓ cup grated Parmesan cheese

⅓ cup chopped fresh basil

INSTRUCTIONS

1. The day before serving, prepare the yogurt "cheese." Mix the yogurt with ½ teaspoon of the salt in a small bowl. Line a strainer with several layers of cheesecloth, then transfer the yogurt to the strainer.

2. Squeeze the cloth very gently around the yogurt and place the strainer over a bowl. Refrigerate and let drain for at least 10 hours.

3. When ready to continue with the recipe, carefully remove the cheesecloth from the ball of cheese. Preheat the oven to 425°F.

4. Bring the water to a boil in a saucepan and stir the polenta into the boiling water.

5. Add remaining ½ teaspoon salt, then reduce the heat to low, cover, and cook, stirring frequently, for 15 minutes or until thick and soft.

6. Pour the polenta into a 9-inch nonstick pie plate or casserole dish and spread evenly over the bottom and up the sides.

7. Spread the pizza sauce over the polenta.

8. Arrange the onion, tomato, bell pepper, and mushrooms over the sauce, then top with the yogurt cheese, capers and Parmesan cheese. Bake for 25 minutes or until the pie is bubbling hot throughout.

9. Remove from the oven and top with the basil before slicing and serving.

NUTRITION DATA FOR 1 SERVING:

Calories **272kcal**
Total Carbohydrates **35g**
Protein **18g**
Total Fat **7g**
Saturated Fat **4g**
Polyunsaturated Fat **1g**
Monounsaturated Fat **1g**
Trans Fat **1g**
Cholesterol **23mg**
Sodium **1412mg**
Potassium **749mg**
Dietary Fiber **9g**
Sugars **13g**
Vitamin A **52% Daily Value**
Vitamin C **192% Daily Value**
Calcium **18% Daily Value**
Iron **31% Daily Value**

Portuguese Chorizo Soup

Serves: 6

This is an excellent comforting soup that is full of flavor, vibrant in color and perfect for the colder months. The chorizo sausage is certainly the star of the recipe, giving the dish a wonderfully spicy flavor, while the potato is a rustic and hearty addition.

Make a double batch of this soup if you can, and freeze half so that you have a ready-made meal for those nights you can't be bothered to cook.

INGREDIENTS

2 tbsp. olive oil

1 cup diced onion

2 tsp. minced garlic

8 oz. chorizo sausage, thinly sliced

2 cups peeled, sliced potatoes

4 cups chicken stock

4 cups water

½ lb. kale, stemmed and sliced

½ lb. green beans, trimmed and sliced

salt and pepper, to taste

INSTRUCTIONS

1. Heat the olive oil in a medium to large soup pot over medium heat. Add the onions and garlic and cook 2–3 minutes, until soft and transparent (don't allow them to brown).

2. Add the chorizo and potatoes and sauté for 5 to10 minutes more, or until the potatoes are slightly golden and the sausage is browned.

3. Pour in the stock and water and bring to a boil. Cook at a gentle boil over medium heat for 15 minutes.

4. Add the kale and green beans, reduce the heat to low, and simmer, uncovered, for 5 minutes.

5. Season with salt and pepper, to taste, and ladle into bowls and serve.

NUTRITION DATA FOR 1 SERVING:

Calories **309kcal**
Total Carbohydrates **28g**
Protein **12g**
Total Fat **17g**
Saturated Fat **5g**
Polyunsaturated Fat **1g**
Monounsaturated Fat **4g**
Trans Fat **0.8g**
Cholesterol **23mg**
Sodium **899mg**
Potassium **692mg**
Dietary Fiber **6g**
Sugars **3g**
Vitamin A **132% Daily Value**
Vitamin C **122% Daily Value**
Calcium **13% Daily Value**
Iron **15% Daily Value**

Roasted Lamb Rack with Velvet Black Olive Sauce

Serves: 4

This roasted rack of lamb with velvety olive sauce is a dish you'll want to bring out when you have a big impression to make.

The lamb melts in your mouth perfectly and pairs wonderfully with the rich, smooth and dreamy black olive sauce. The sauce takes a little time to prepare, so pour yourself a glass of wine and enjoy your moment in the kitchen, cooking with love and knowing you're about to create a masterpiece your dinner guests will cherish.

INGREDIENTS

FOR THE SAUCE:

½ cup unsalted butter

4 cloves garlic, peeled and crushed

4 shallots, peeled and chopped

1 tbsp. black peppercorns

2 cups Madeira wine

2 cups red wine

1 medium tomato, diced

1 small rosemary sprig

1 cup demi-glace (or good-quality lamb or beef broth)

½ cup pitted Niçoise olives

salt and pepper, to taste

FOR THE LAMB:

2 lamb racks, 8 chops on each

1 tbsp. olive oil, plus more for the pan

2 tsp. salt

2 tsp. black pepper

1 rosemary sprig, leaves only, chopped

INSTRUCTIONS

1. Preheat the oven to 350°F.

FOR THE SAUCE:

2. To make the sauce, heat 1 tablespoon of the butter in a large skillet over medium heat. Add the garlic, shallots and peppercorns and sauté until lightly browned.

3. Add the Madeira, red wine, tomato and rosemary.

4. Simmer until reduced by two-thirds, leaving approximately 1 cup total, about 30 minutes.

5. Add the demi-glace and bring to a boil. Whisk in the remaining butter a little at a time until it is incorporated. (If you would like a thicker, richer sauce, simply add a little more butter.)

6. Strain the sauce through a fine-mesh strainer, then transfer to a blender.

7. Add half the olives and purée until almost smooth.

8. Roughly chop the remaining olives, add to the sauce and stir to mix.

9. Season with salt and pepper, to taste, then set aside in a warm place until serving time.

FOR THE LAMB:

10. To make the lamb, rub each rack well with the olive oil and season with the salt, pepper and rosemary.

11. Heat a roasting pan or large sauté pan over high heat until very hot.

12. Add a few drops of oil to the pan, then add the lamb racks and sear on all sides until brown.

recipe continues

13. Turn the racks bone side down in the hot pan and transfer to the oven. Roast to your desired doneness, 10–15 minutes for medium-rare.

14. Allow the lamb to rest for 10 minutes, then slice into 8 chops per rack.

15. Serve 4 chops on each plate, accompanied by the sauce. We suggest serving these with garlic mashed potatoes and lightly cooked vegetables.

NUTRITION DATA FOR 1 SERVING:

Calories **1247kcal**	Sodium **1656mg**
Total Carbohydrates **29g**	Potassium **384mg**
Protein **88g**	Dietary Fiber **1g**
Total Fat **61g**	Sugars **12g**
Saturated Fat **26g**	Vitamin A **22% Daily Value**
Polyunsaturated Fat **4g**	Vitamin C **12% Daily Value**
Monounsaturated Fat **23g**	Calcium **9% Daily Value**
Trans Fat **0.5g**	Iron **44% Daily Value**
Cholesterol **340mg**	

Serves: 4

Try to source the freshest local squid available, as this will provide the best flavor. If fresh squid is not available, you can also make this recipe using large frozen squid tubes; thaw the squid before beginning the recipe.

This dish is bursting with wonderful fresh flavors from all the herbs, along with an underlying sweetness from the currants. Keep this recipe up your sleeve for the next time you want to wow your dinner guests.

Stuffed Baked Squid

INGREDIENTS

4 large fresh large squid (about 3 lb.)

¼ cup olive oil

1 cup coarsely chopped onion

⅓ cup long-grain rice

⅓ cup pine nuts

2 large cloves garlic, chopped

¼ cup currants

1 cup dry red wine

¼ cup water, plus more as needed

salt and freshly ground black pepper, to taste

¾ cup chopped fresh parsley

¼ cup chopped fresh dill

¼ cup chopped fresh mint

2 cups canned diced tomatoes

INSTRUCTIONS

1. Preheat the oven to 350°F.

2. Wash and clean each squid. Grasp the head just below the eyes and pull it off from the rest of the body; set aside.

3. Cut away the thin purplish membrane on the outside of the tail section. Using your index finger, scoop out and discard the guts and thin cartilage "icicle" on the inside of the tail section. Rinse the tail sections inside and out and set aside in a colander to drain.

4. Take the head section in one hand and put pressure with your thumb and forefinger around the mouth and eyes to squeeze them out. Discard the mouth and eyes.

5. Chop the squid tentacles and set aside. These will be used in the stuffing.

6. Heat 2 tablespoons of the olive oil in a large skillet over medium heat. Add the onion and sauté until soft, about 5–6 minutes.

7. Add the rice, tentacles and pine nuts and sauté 2–3 minutes

8. Add the garlic and currants and stir quickly with a wooden spoon.

recipe continues

9. Pour in ¼ cup of the wine and ¼ cup of the water. Season with salt and pepper to taste. Reduce the heat to low and simmer, covered, for about 10 minutes, then add the parsley, dill and mint. Cover and continue to cook about 5 minutes more, until the liquid is almost completely absorbed and the rice is soft but only about half cooked. Remove from the heat and let cool.

10. When the rice is cool enough to handle, use a small teaspoon or a butter knife to carefully fill about three-quarters of each squid with the rice mixture.

11. Use toothpicks to hold the squid securely closed.

12. Pour the remaining 2 tablespoons olive oil into a large casserole dish.

13. Place the squid carefully in the dish and pour in the remaining ¾ cup wine and the canned tomatoes. If the squid are not fully submerged, add just enough water to cover, then season with salt and pepper to taste.

14. Cover and place in the oven to cook for 1½ to 2 hours or until the rice is cooked and the squid is fork-tender.

15. Check throughout the cooking time to see if more water is necessary so that the mixture doesn't dry out.

16. Serve the squid with a simple green salad.

NUTRITION DATA FOR 1 SERVING:

Calories **558kcal**
Total Carbohydrates **25g**
Protein **43g**
Total Fat **26g**
Saturated Fat **4g**
Polyunsaturated Fat **7g**
Monounsaturated Fat **13g**
Trans Fat **0.8g**
Cholesterol **583mg**
Sodium **323mg**
Potassium **1074mg**
Dietary Fiber **3g**
Sugars **6g**
Vitamin A **17% Daily Value**
Vitamin C **57% Daily Value**
Calcium **13% Daily Value**
Iron **21% Daily Value**

Turkey Barley Soup

Serves: 4

If you're looking for a no-fuss recipe that can easily use up leftovers, this one is for you. Don't let your leftover turkey meat go to waste—instead turn it into a fabulous soup with vegetables and barley. If you don't have turkey left over, chicken is also a great option here. The barley in this soup balances out the celery and carrot well, while the parsley gives this soup a lovely fresh flavor.

You can make this dish on the stovetop or in a slow cooker, so there is minimal effort required. Using the slow cooker makes this a great "set it and forget it" dinner: you can put your soup on to cook in the morning, walk out the door and come home to an aroma-filled kitchen that will smell absolutely delicious!

INGREDIENTS

8 cups chicken stock

1½ cups diced cooked turkey breast

1 cup pearl barley

1 onion, chopped

2 stalks celery, chopped

3 carrots, sliced

1 bay leaf

1 tsp. dry thyme

¼ tsp. dried marjoram

¼ tsp. ground black pepper

2 tbsp. chopped fresh parsley

salt and pepper, to taste

INSTRUCTIONS

1. Combine all the ingredients in a large soup pot over medium heat or in a slow cooker.

2. Cook in the slow cooker on low for 6 hours, or simmer on the stove covered for 1 hour, until the carrots are tender and the barley is soft.

3. Ladle the soup into four serving bowls, season with salt and pepper, to taste, and serve with warm crusty bread if desired.

NUTRITION DATA FOR 1 SERVING:

Calories **294kcal**	Sodium **81mg**
Total Carbohydrates **51g**	Potassium **632mg**
Protein **19g**	Dietary Fiber **10g**
Total Fat **3g**	Sugars **5g**
Saturated Fat **0.4g**	Vitamin A **172% Daily Value**
Polyunsaturated Fat **0.3g**	Vitamin C **11% Daily Value**
Monounsaturated Fat **0.3g**	Calcium **6% Daily Value**
Trans Fat **0.3g**	Iron **14% Daily Value**
Cholesterol **32mg**	

Tuscan White Bean Stew

Serves: 6

Surprisingly full of flavor considering the simple ingredients and the lack of effort required, this quick and easy stew is ready for you to devour within 20 minutes. It's the perfect mid- or late-week dinner (or for any other occasion you may be short on time).

Feel free to play around with this recipe by using different varieties of beans or adding in some leafy greens like kale or chard. If you prefer a little spice, adjust the chili flakes and paprika to taste.

INGREDIENTS

1 tbsp. olive oil

2 anchovy fillets, chopped

1 tsp. minced garlic

½ tsp. paprika

½ tsp. crushed red pepper

1 cup shredded or diced cabbage

1 large green bell pepper, seeded and chopped

1 (14-oz.) can crushed tomatoes

1½ cups canned white beans, drained and rinsed

1 cup chicken broth

2 tsp. freshly squeezed lemon juice

4 oz. pasta (such as farfalle)

salt and pepper, to taste

freshly chopped oregano

freshly chopped parsley

INSTRUCTIONS

1. Heat the oil in a large saucepan over medium-high heat.
2. Stir in the anchovies, garlic, paprika and crushed red pepper and heat for approximately 30 seconds.
3. Add the cabbage and bell pepper and sauté for another 1 to 2 minutes until the cabbage is slightly limp.
4. Add the crushed tomatoes, beans, broth and lemon juice.
5. Reduce the heat to medium-low and allow to simmer, uncovered, 10–15 minutes.
6. Meanwhile, cook the pasta according to the package directions.
7. Divide the hot pasta among 6 bowls and spoon the stew over the top. Season with salt and black pepper to taste. Garnish with chopped oregano and parsley.

NUTRITION DATA FOR 1 SERVING:

Calories **168kcal**	Sodium **539mg**
Total Carbohydrates **27g**	Potassium **312mg**
Protein **9g**	Dietary Fiber **7g**
Total Fat **3g**	Sugars **1g**
Saturated Fat **1g**	Vitamin A **14% Daily Value**
Polyunsaturated Fat **1g**	Vitamin C **55% Daily Value**
Monounsaturated Fat **2g**	Calcium **10% Daily Value**
Trans Fat **3g**	Iron **18% Daily Value**
Cholesterol **3mg**	

Drink

RECIPES

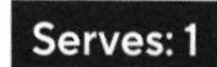

This vitamin-boosting smoothie is perfect for a hot afternoon. And the best part? It's incredibly easy to make!

Sun Smoothie

INGREDIENTS

1 cup almond milk

½ cup orange juice

¼ cup wheat germ

1 banana

INSTRUCTIONS

Combine all four ingredients in a blender. Blend on high until smooth. Serve immediately.

NUTRITION DATA FOR 1 SERVING:

Calories **140kcal**
Total Carbohydrates **98g**
Protein **2g**
Total Fat **0g**
Saturated Fat **0g**
Polyunsaturated Fat **0g**
Monounsaturated Fat **0g**
Trans Fat **0g**
Cholesterol **0mg**
Sodium **5mg**
Potassium **2mg**
Dietary Fiber **4g**
Sugars **85g**
Vitamin A **5% Daily Value**
Vitamin C **9.4% Daily Value**
Calcium **2.6% Daily Value**
Iron **3.8% Daily Value**

Serves: 1

This cold, sweet drink is full of nutrients and is perfect for a nice summer day!

Frosty Fruit Smoothie

INGREDIENTS

1 banana

1 cup frozen strawberries

1 cup orange juice

mint leaves (optional)

INSTRUCTIONS

Combine all the ingredients into a blender and purée on high speed. Serve immediately, topped with a mint leaf, if desired.

NUTRITION DATA FOR 1 SERVING:

Calories **120kcal**	Sodium **15mg**
Total Carbohydrates **28.8g**	Potassium **8mg**
Protein **1.4g**	Dietary Fiber **0g**
Total Fat **0g**	Sugars **27g**
Saturated Fat **0g**	Vitamin A **10% Daily Value**
Polyunsaturated Fat **0g**	Vitamin C **6.3% Daily Value**
Monounsaturated Fat **0g**	Calcium **2.4% Daily Value**
Trans Fat **0g**	Iron **1.8% Daily Value**
Cholesterol **0mg**	

Serves: 3

The perfect drink for those hot summer days on the beach! The sparkling water and herbs give it just the perfect punch of freshness.

Sugar-Free Blueberry Lemonade

INGREDIENTS

1½ cups fresh lemon juice

½ cup powdered stevia (sugar substitute)

6 cups water

1 cup cold sparkling water

1 cup blueberries, plus more for garnish

¼ cup mixed fresh herbs, such as basil, mint and tarragon, plus more for garnish

INSTRUCTIONS

Pour the lemon juice into a pitcher and stir in the stevia until dissolved. Add the water and sparkling water and stir well. Mash the blueberries and herbs in a bowl with a wooden spoon. Divide the blueberry mixture among 3 or 4 cups and pour the lemonade over the top. Garnish each glass with whole blueberries and mint.

NUTRITION DATA FOR 1 SERVING:

Calories **110kcal**	Sodium **50mg**
Total Carbohydrates **2.8g**	Potassium **29mg**
Protein **21.4g**	Dietary Fiber **1g**
Total Fat **0g**	Sugars **0g**
Saturated Fat **0g**	Vitamin A **3.4% Daily Value**
Polyunsaturated Fat **0g**	Vitamin C **5.2% Daily Value**
Monounsaturated Fat **0g**	Calcium **3.6% Daily Value**
Trans Fat **0g**	Iron **8.3% Daily Value**
Cholesterol **0mg**	

Serves: 2

One of the most popular smoothies. Silky smooth from the Banana and Almonds with just a hint of acid from the Greek Yogurt, finished off with fresh mint!

Greek Yogurt Smoothie

INGREDIENTS

⅓ cup Greek yogurt

½ ripe banana, frozen

⅓ cup blueberries, frozen, plus more for garnish

½ cup spinach, frozen

¼ cup almond milk

mint leaves (optional)

INSTRUCTIONS

Combine all the ingredients in a blender and blend until smooth and creamy. Serve immediately, garnished with extra berries and a sprig of mint, if desired.

NUTRITION DATA FOR 1 SERVING:

Calories **280kcal**
Total Carbohydrates **1g**
Protein **12g**
Total Fat **1g**
Saturated Fat **0.4g**
Polyunsaturated Fat **0.1g**
Monounsaturated Fat **0.3g**
Trans Fat **0.1g**
Cholesterol **10mg**
Sodium **90mg**
Potassium **65mg**
Dietary Fiber **4g**
Sugars **22g**
Vitamin A **6.3% Daily Value**
Vitamin C **2.8% Daily Value**
Calcium **4.6% Daily Value**
Iron **5.7% Daily Value**

Serves: 6

A great vitamin packed way to finish off that late night movie at the end of the week.

Date Horchata

INGREDIENTS

6 cups water

1 cup white rice

½ cup dates

1½ tsp. vanilla extract

1 cinnamon stick

1 tbsp. maple syrup (optional)

1 cup almond milk

INSTRUCTIONS

1. Heat 2 cups of the water until it is hot, but not quite boiling. Add the rice and soak in the hot water for 2 hours. The rice should be soft, but still raw. Drain and transfer the rice to a blender. Add the remaining 4 cups of water, the dates, vanilla and cinnamon. Blend for about 1 minute. Test for sweetness, and add more dates or maple syrup as needed.

2. Pour the mixture through a cheesecloth into a bowl; discard the pulp. Stir in the almond milk and whisk until well combined. Transfer to a serving pitcher. Serve immediately over ice.

NUTRITION DATA FOR 1 SERVING:

Calories **83kcal**	Sodium **75mg**
Total Carbohydrates **20g**	Potassium **38mg**
Protein **1g**	Dietary Fiber **4g**
Total Fat **2g**	Sugars **2g**
Saturated Fat **1g**	Vitamin A **5.2% Daily Value**
Polyunsaturated Fat **1g**	Vitamin C **4.8% Daily Value**
Monounsaturated Fat **1g**	Calcium **6.8 % Daily Value**
Trans Fat **1g**	Iron **3.7% Daily Value**
Cholesterol **0mg**	

Snack

RECIPES

Makes: 1 Pie (12 slices)

This is a family-proven spanakopita recipe! This delicious, salty Greek cake is made from perfectly crispy layers of phyllo dough and a nice filling of spinach and feta cheese.

Greek Spinach Pie (Spanakopita)

INGREDIENTS

FOR THE FILLING:

16 oz. frozen chopped spinach, thawed and well drained

2 bunches flat-leaf parsley, stems trimmed, finely chopped

1 large yellow onion, finely chopped

2 cloves, minced

10.5 oz. feta cheese, crumbled

4 eggs

2 tbsp. extra-virgin olive oil

2 tsp. dried dill weed

freshly ground black pepper

INSTRUCTIONS

1. Preheat the oven to 325°F.
2. Drain the spinach well and squeeze out any excess liquid with your hands, then transfer to a medium bowl.
3. Add all the remaining filling ingredients and stir until well combined.
4. Unroll the phyllo sheets and place them between two slightly damp kitchen cloths.
5. Brush the bottom and sides of a 9½-by-13-inch baking dish with the olive oil.
6. Line the baking dish with two sheets of phyllo, allowing them to cover the sides of the dish. Brush with more olive oil. Add two more sheets of phyllo, and brush them with olive oil. Repeat until two-thirds of the phyllo have been used up.
7. Next, evenly distribute the spinach and feta filling over the phyllo. Top with two more sheets, and brush with olive oil.
8. Continuously layer the phyllo sheets two at a time, brushing with olive oil, until you've used up all the sheets. Brush the very top layer with olive oil, and sprinkle with just a few drops of water.

FOR THE CRUST:

1 (16-oz.) package Phyllo pastry, thawed according to package directions

1 cup extra-virgin olive oil, or more if needed

9. Fold the flaps (if necessary) and remove excess from the sides—you can crumble them a little. Brush the folded sides well with olive oil.

10. Bake for 1 hour, or until the phyllo crust is crisp and golden brown. Remove from the oven. Let stand for 5 minutes, then cut into squares and serve.

NUTRITION DATA FOR 1 SERVING:

Calories **393kcal**	Sodium **290mg**
Total Carbohydrates **38g**	Potassium **141mg**
Protein **21g**	Dietary Fiber **1g**
Total Fat **20g**	Sugars **0g**
Saturated Fat **3g**	Vitamin A **8% Daily Value**
Trans Fat **0g**	Vitamin C **5% Daily Value**
Polyunsaturated Fat **2g**	Calcium **36% Daily Value**
Monounsaturated Fat **3g**	Iron **3% Daily Value**
Cholesterol **35mg**	

Serves: 8

This recipe will teach you how to make hummus like a professional! No mezze is complete without a bowl of hummus and some warm pita, but there are many other ways to enjoy this delicious dip too! For example it's amazing as a sandwich spread!

Classic Lemon Hummus

INGREDIENTS

3 cups cooked, peeled chickpeas

1–2 cloves garlic, minced

3–4 ice cubes

⅓ cup tahini paste

½ tsp. kosher salt

1 lemon, juiced

hot water (if needed)

early-harvest, extra-virgin olive oil

ground sumac powder, to taste

INSTRUCTIONS

1. Combine the chickpeas and garlic in the bowl of a food processor. Purée until a smooth, powderlike mixture forms.

2. With the processor running, add the ice cubes, tahini paste, salt, and lemon juice. Blend for about 4 minutes. If the consistency is still too thick, slowly add a little hot water with the processor running, and blend until you reach the desired silky-smooth consistency.

3. Spread the hummus into a serving bowl and add a generous drizzle of oil. Place a few chickpeas in the middle, if desired. Sprinkle the sumac powder on top. Enjoy with warm pita wedges and your favorite vegetables. Store in the refrigerator for up to 5 days, if desired.

NUTRITION DATA FOR 1 SERVING:

Calories **176kcal**
Total Carbohydrates **19g**
Protein **7g**
Total Fat **9g**
Saturated Fat **4g**
Monounsaturated Fat **1g**
Polyunsaturated Fat **0.7g**
Trans Fat **3g**
Cholesterol **0.0mg**
Sodium **153mg**
Potassium **74mg**
Dietary Fiber **0.9g**
Sugars **3g**
Vitamin A **4% Daily Value**
Vitamin C **6% Daily Value**
Calcium **17% Daily Value**
Iron **13% Daily Value**

Smooth Tzatziki

Serves: 3

This authentic tzatziki recipe comes from the Greek island of Paros. Tzatziki is a creamy Greek yogurt sauce with cucumbers and fresh garlic. It is a versatile sauce that is the perfect side to many Mediterranean dishes. You can also top your sandwiches with it, or just use it as a dip with warm pita and your favorite vegetables!

INGREDIENTS

⅓ English cucumber, partially peeled (striped) and sliced

1 tsp. kosher salt, divided

4 to 5 cloves garlic, peeled and finely grated or minced (you can use less if you prefer)

1 tbsp. extra-virgin olive oil, plus more for serving

1 tsp. white vinegar

2 cups Greek yogurt

¼ tsp. ground white pepper

INSTRUCTIONS

1. Grate the cucumbers in a food processor, then toss with ½ teaspoon of the salt. Transfer to a fine-mesh strainer over a deep bowl to drain, about 10 minutes. Spoon the grated cucumber into a piece of cheesecloth or a double-thickness napkin and squeeze dry. Set aside.

2. In a large mixing bowl, combine the garlic with the remaining ½ teaspoon of salt, the olive oil and the vinegar. Mix to combine evenly.

3. Add the grated cucumber to the large bowl with the garlic mixture. Stir in the yogurt and white pepper. Combine thoroughly, then cover tightly and refrigerate for a couple of hours.

4. When ready to serve, stir the tzatziki to refresh, and transfer to a serving bowl. Drizzle with more extra-virgin olive oil, if desired. Add a side of warm pita bread and your favorite vegetables. Enjoy!

NUTRITION DATA FOR 1 SERVING:

Calories **34kcal**	Sodium **209mg**
Total Carbohydrates **1g**	Potassium **156mg**
Protein **1g**	Dietary Fiber **1g**
Fat **1g**	Sugars **1g**
Saturated Fat **1g**	Vitamin A **9% Daily Value**
Polyunsaturated Fat **1g**	Vitamin C **11% Daily Value**
Monounsaturated Fat **1g**	Calcium **29% Daily Value**
Trans Fat **01g**	Iron **10% Daily Value**
Cholesterol **10mg**	

Serves: 5

You'll love this authentic recipe for tahini sauce with garlic, lime juice and fresh parsley! This rich vegan sauce is popular in the Mediterranean and the Middle East, and can elevate any meal, from kebabs to falafel sandwiches and everything in between. It's also perfect served as part of a mezze with warm pita and fresh vegetables!

Tahini Sauce

INGREDIENTS

1–2 cloves garlic

½ tsp. salt

⅓ cup tahini paste

½ cup freshly squeezed lime juice (or lemon juice, if you prefer)

1 cup chopped fresh parsley leaves (optional)

INSTRUCTIONS

1. Using a mortar and pestle, crush the garlic cloves with the salt into a paste. Alternatively, you can mince the garlic, and season with salt.
2. Add the crushed garlic, tahini paste and lime juice to the bowl of a food processor and blend (it will become thick as it emulsifies). If the mixture is too thick, add a little bit of water and blend again until you reach the desired consistency.
3. Transfer the tahini to a serving bowl and stir in the parsley, if using. Enjoy!

NUTRITION DATA FOR 1 SERVING:

Calories **57kcal**
Total Carbohydrates **5g**
Protein **1g**
Total Fat **4g**
Saturated Fat **1g**
Polyunsaturated Fat **1g**
Monounsaturated Fat **1g**
Trans Fat **1g**
Cholesterol **0mg**
Sodium **99mg**
Potassium **48mg**
Dietary Fiber **1g**
Sugars **1g**
Vitamin A **11% Daily Value**
Vitamin C **13% Daily Value**
Calcium **38% Daily Value**
Iron **20% Daily Value**

Homemade Tahini Paste

Yield: ½ cup

This authentic Homemade Tahini Paste is the base to the hummus recipes that go along in this book! It's always a good idea to have it on hand! The dish can be stored in the refrigerator for up to a week.

INGREDIENTS

½ cup hulled sesame seeds

2–4 tbsp. olive oil

pinch of salt

INSTRUCTIONS

Grind the sesame seeds in a food processor and gradually add the oil until smooth. Mix in a pinch of salt.

Tip: Lightly toast the seeds in a dry pan on the stovetop before grinding for a deeper, nutty flavor. Don't toast the seeds in the oven as they can easily burn.

NUTRITION DATA FOR 1 TABLESPOON:

Calories **59kcal**	Sodium **290mg**
Total Carbohydrates **2g**	Potassium **141mg**
Protein **1g**	Dietary Fiber **1g**
Total Fat **6g**	Sugars **0g**
Saturated Fat **1g**	Vitamin A **4.8% Daily Value**
Polyunsaturated Fat **2g**	Vitamin C **2.5% Daily Value**
Monounsaturated Fat **3g**	Calcium **2.6% Daily Value**
Trans Fat **0g**	Iron **5.3% Daily Value**
Cholesterol **35mg**	

The perfect snack! Healthy, filling, and offering so many different ways and flavors to play with, it can be served with your favorite veggies or bread.

Creamy Tahini Hummus

INGREDIENTS

¼ cup tahini paste

¼ cup lemon juice (from 1 large lemon)

2 tbsp. olive oil, plus more for serving

1 clove garlic

½ tsp. cumin

½ tsp. salt

1½ cups canned or cooked chickpeas, peeled and rinsed

2–3 tbsp. water, as needed

dash of paprika

INSTRUCTIONS

Combine the tahini and lemon juice in the bowl of a food processor and pulse to mix. Add the olive oil, garlic, cumin and salt and pulse until mixed. Add the chickpeas and pulse again until smooth. If the hummus is too thick, add the water a little at a time until you reach the desired consistency. Serve with a drizzle of olive oil and sprinkle the paprika over the top. Use veggies to dip!

NUTRITION DATA FOR 1 SERVING (¼ CUP):

Calories **89kcal**	Sodium **18mg**
Total Carbohydrates **4g**	Potassium **8mg**
Protein **3g**	Dietary Fiber **2g**
Total Fat **9g**	Sugars **0g**
Saturated Fat **3g**	Vitamin A **1.3% Daily Value**
Polyunsaturated Fat **2g**	Vitamin C **3.5% Daily Value**
Monounsaturated Fat **3g**	Calcium **2.6% Daily Value**
Trans Fat **0g**	Iron **1.3% Daily Value**
Cholesterol **35mg**	

Beetroot Hummus

Yield:
1½ cups

Sweet but just a little tart, the perfect way to introduce some extra flavor by roasting some beetroot and garlic.

INGREDIENTS

1 red beet

2 cloves garlic, peeled

2 tbsp. olive oil

1½ cups cooked or canned chickpeas, drained and rinsed

3 tbsp. warm water

2 tbsp. tahini paste

2 tbsp. lemon juice

½ tsp. cumin

½ tsp. coriander

salt and black pepper, to taste

INSTRUCTIONS

1. Preheat the oven to 400°F.

2. Place the beet and garlic cloves on a piece of foil and drizzle with the olive oil. Fold the foil over and seal into a packet, then place on a baking sheet. Transfer to the oven and roast for 30 minutes or until the beet is fork-tender. Carefully open the foil packet and let cool. When cool enough to handle, remove the beet skin. Place the beet and garlic cloves in the bowl of a food processor and blend. Continue blending while adding the rest of the ingredients for about 5 minutes. Keep in the fridge until ready to use. Serve with veggies!

NUTRITION DATA FOR 1 SERVING (¼ CUP):

Calories **60kcal**	Sodium **93mg**
Total Carbohydrates **7g**	Potassium **14mg**
Protein **3g**	Dietary Fiber **1g**
Total Fat **3g**	Sugars **2g**
Saturated Fat **1g**	Vitamin A **6.1% Daily Value**
Polyunsaturated Fat **1g**	Vitamin C **5.8% Daily Value**
Monounsaturated Fat **1g**	Calcium **3.2% Daily Value**
Trans Fat **0g**	Iron **5% Daily Value**
Cholesterol **12mg**	

Makes: 1 large salad or 2 small salads (2 servings)

The perfect snack for movie night! High in Iron and Potassium and only takes a few minutes to make. Add some feta for some added texture.

Chickpea Salad

INGREDIENTS

FOR THE SALAD:

1 can (15 oz.) chickpeas,

½ cup sun-dried tomatoes

½ cucumber, diced

½ cup diced red onion

½ cup sliced olives

¼ cup parsley, chopped

¼ cup crumbled feta cheese

FOR THE DRESSING:

¼ cup olive oil

2 tbsp. red wine vinegar

½ tsp. cumin

salt and black pepper, to taste

INSTRUCTIONS

1. Drain the can of chickpeas and transfer to a large bowl. Add the sun-dried tomatoes, cucumbers, onions, olives, parsley and feta cheese and stir to mix.

2. Combine all the dressing ingredients in a bowl. Refrigerate both the salad and the dressing for an hour before combining and serving.

NUTRITION DATA FOR 1 SERVING:

Calories **166kcal**
Total Carbohydrates **20g**
Protein **4g**
Total Fat **8g**
Saturated Fat **1g**
Polyunsaturated Fat **1g**
Monounsaturated Fat **5g**
Trans Fat **0g**
Cholesterol **0mg**
Sodium **253mg**
Potassium **234mg**
Dietary Fiber **4g**
Sugars **0g**
Vitamin A **1.5% Daily Value**
Vitamin C **4.8% Daily Value**
Calcium **3.8% Daily Value**
Iron **7.1% Daily Value**

Apple Slices with Almond Butter

Serves: 1

This little treat might look simple but it packs a punch, 34% of your daily Calcium and 19% of your daily Iron!

INGREDIENTS

1 apple

¼ cup almond butter

2 tbsp. sliced almonds

2 tbsp. walnuts

¼ cup dark chocolate chips

INSTRUCTIONS

Slice the apple crosswise. Spread each slice with almond butter and top with the almonds, walnuts and dark chocolate chips.

NUTRITION DATA FOR 1 SERVING:

Calories **258kcal**
Total Carbohydrates **17g**
Protein **21g**
Total Fat **56g**
Saturated Fat **4g**
Polyunsaturated Fat **14g**
Monounsaturated Fat **30g**
Trans Fat **2g**
Cholesterol **0mg**
Sodium **7mg**
Potassium **8mg**
Dietary Fiber **10g**
Sugars **4.4g**
Vitamin A **0% Daily Value**
Vitamin C **0% Daily Value**
Calcium **34% Daily Value**
Iron **19% Daily Value**

Serves: 1

Starting with some plain Greek yogurt, simply throw in your favorite fresh berries, and you'll have a delicious and nutritious snack.

Plain Greek Yogurt and Fresh Berries

INGREDIENTS

1 cup plain Greek yogurt

½ cup mixed berries (such as strawberries, blueberries or raspberries)

mint leaves (optional)

½ cup rolled oats

INSTRUCTIONS

Top the yogurt with your favorite berries and mint. Sprinkle rolled oats over top and add almonds for a flavor booster if desired

NUTRITION DATA FOR 1 SERVING:

Calories **220kcal**	Sodium **115mg**
Total Carbohydrates **37g**	Potassium **78mg**
Protein **14g**	Dietary Fiber **3g**
Total Fat **4g**	Sugars **2g**
Saturated Fat **1g**	Vitamin A **3.7% Daily Value**
Polyunsaturated Fat **2g**	Vitamin C **2.5% Daily Value**
Monounsaturated Fat **1g**	Calcium **6.6% Daily Value**
Trans Fat **0g**	Iron **6.3% Daily Value**
Cholesterol **5mg**	

Dessert

RECIPES

Serves: 4

Your friends and family will love my tiramisu recipe. It's easy to make, and I guarantee it will be the best tiramisu you've ever had! The mascarpone does not have to be at room temperature, but it will be easier to mix in if it is. Take it out of the refrigerator as you gather the other ingredients to make the recipe.

Mediterranean Tiramisu

INGREDIENTS

6 large egg yolks (approx. ½ cup of yolks)

1 cup sugar

1¼ cups mascarpone cheese, room temperature

1⅓ cups heavy whipping cream

1 cup cold espresso or strong coffee

½ cup coffee-flavored liqueur (optional)

30 Italian ladyfingers, Savoiardi style (about 1½ 7-oz. packages)

1 oz. unsweetened cocoa for dusting

INSTRUCTIONS

1. Combine the egg yolks and sugar in the top of a double boiler, set over boiling water and use a wire whisk to mix. Reduce the heat to low and cook, stirring constantly with the whisk, for about 10 minutes. This is your sabayon. Remove from the heat and continue to whisk until the yolks are thick and lemon-colored. Allow to cool briefly.
2. Add the room-temperature mascarpone cheese to the whipped yolks and whisk until well combined.
3. In a separate bowl, use an electric hand mixer or a stand mixer to whip the cream to stiff peaks.
4. Gently fold the whipped cream into the mascarpone-sabayon mixture and set aside.
5. Mix the cold espresso with the coffee liqueur, if using. Dip the ladyfingers into the mixture just long enough to get them wet. Do not soak them!
6. Arrange half of the ladyfingers in the bottom of a 9-inch-square baking dish or other similar-size container.
7. Spoon half the mascarpone cream filling over the ladyfingers.
8. Repeat the process with another layer of ladyfingers, and add another layer of mascarpone cream.

9. Dust the top with unsweetened cocoa and refrigerate for at least 4 hours, or ideally overnight.

NUTRITION DATA FOR 1 SERVING:

Calories **490kcal**	Sodium **200mg**
Total Carbohydrates **37g**	Potassium **176mg**
Protein **5g**	Dietary Fiber **10g**
Total Fat **34g**	Sugars **5g**
Saturated Fat **10g**	Vitamin A **7% Daily Value**
Polyunsaturated Fat **6g**	Vitamin C **12% Daily Value**
Monounsaturated Fat **14g**	Calcium **25% Daily Value**
Trans Fat **4g**	Iron **18% Daily Value**
Cholesterol **20mg**	

Greek-Style No-Bake Cheesecake with Yogurt

Serves: 4

Everyone can enjoy this delicious and easy Greek-style, no-bake cheesecake recipe! It's creamy, rich and refreshing, with a crunchy biscuit base and a delicious jam topping. Perfect to finish off a nice summers day!

INGREDIENTS

4 tbsp. butter, melted, plus more for the pan

1 (9-oz.) pkg. digestive biscuits

16 oz. cream cheese

5 oz. thick Greek yogurt

2 tbsp. honey

1 tsp. vanilla extract

4 oz. powdered sugar

9.5 oz. heavy cream

½ to 1 cup jam of your choice

INSTRUCTIONS

1. To make the base, butter a 9-inch removable-bottom pie tin. Place the biscuits in the bowl of a food processor and pulse until only crumbs remain. Transfer the crumbs to a bowl, then pour in the melted butter. Mix thoroughly until the crumbs are completely coated. Pour the mixture into the prepared pie tin and press firmly down into the base in an even layer. Place the tin in the fridge while you make the filling.

2. Combine the cream cheese, Greek yogurt, honey, vanilla and powdered sugar in a bowl, then beat with an electric mixer until smooth. Add the heavy cream and continue beating until the mixture is completely combined.

3. Pour the mixture into the biscuit crust and top the cheesecake with jam, to taste. Refrigerate overnight, or for at least 6 hours. Enjoy!

NUTRITION DATA FOR 1 SERVING:

Calories **402kcal**	Sodium **400mg**
Total Carbohydrates **36g**	Potassium **348mg**
Protein **5g**	Dietary Fiber **0g**
Total Fat **9g**	Sugars **9g**
Saturated Fat **4g**	Vitamin A **13% Daily Value**
Polyunsaturated Fat **2g**	Vitamin C **9% Daily Value**
Monounsaturated Fat **3g**	Calcium **32% Daily Value**
Trans Fat **2g**	Iron **10% Daily Value**
Cholesterol **36mg**	

Greek Yogurt with Honey & Walnuts (Yiaourti Me Meli)

Serves: 1

This delicious Greek yogurt with honey is sprinkled with walnuts, infused with vanilla, and dusted with fragrant cinnamon! If you have a sweet tooth but are looking for something more nutritious than your usual desserts, this 2-minute, no-bake dessert will amaze you.

INGREDIENTS

1 cup walnuts

½ cup honey

2½ cups Greek yogurt, strained

⅓ tsp. vanilla extract

cinnamon, ground

INSTRUCTIONS

1. Preheat the oven to 350°F.

2. Spread the walnuts in a single layer on a baking sheet and toast 7–8 minutes, or until they turn golden and fragrant. Transfer the toasted walnuts to a bowl, add the honey, and stir to coat. Set aside to cool down, 1–2 minutes.

3. In the meantime, stir together the Greek yogurt and vanilla extract and add to the bowl. Spoon the honey-walnut mixture over the yogurt and sprinkle with cinnamon.

4. Serve immediately or store in the fridge for up to 3 days. Enjoy!

NUTRITION DATA FOR 1 SERVING:

Calories **284kcal**	Sodium **37mg**
Total Carbohydrates **27g**	Potassium **20mg**
Protein **12g**	Dietary Fiber **1g**
Total Fat **15g**	Sugars **24g**
Saturated Fat **4g**	Vitamin A **12% Daily Value**
Polyunsaturated Fat **8g**	Vitamin C **15% Daily Value**
Monounsaturated Fat **4g**	Calcium **22% Daily Value**
Trans Fat **0g**	Iron **19% Daily Value**
Cholesterol **13mg**	

These cookies are airy and crunchy—as well as super quick to bake, so much fun to make and highly addictive to eat! Discover how to prepare them to perfection with this traditional Greek recipe.

Twisty Easter Cookies (Koulourakia)

INGREDIENTS

1 cup butter, chopped, at room temperature

1½ cups sugar

½ cup milk

1½ tbsp. powdered baking ammonia (or baking powder)

4 medium eggs

1 tbsp. vanilla extract

zest of 2 oranges

2¼ lb. all-purpose flour

2 egg yolks

1 tbsp. water

INSTRUCTIONS

1. In a large mixing bowl, combine the butter and sugar in a stand mixer and mix 10–15 minutes, until the butter is creamy and fluffy.

2. In the meantime, warm the milk in a small saucepan until just lukewarm, then remove the pan from the heat. Add the ammonia and blend until dissolved. Set aside.

3. Add the eggs to the butter-sugar mixture one at a time while mixing, allowing time for each one to be incorporated before adding the next. Add the vanilla extract, orange zest and the milk-ammonia mixture and mix to combine. Add the flour a little bit at a time and mix until the ingredients are combined and the dough is soft and not too sticky.

4. Cover the dough with plastic wrap and set aside to rest for 20 minutes.

5. Preheat the oven to 400°F.

6. Turn the dough out onto a clean working surface. Take a small piece of dough and form a log. Twist each end of the koulourakia in opposite directions. Line a large baking sheet with parchment paper and place the koulourakia on the sheet leaving them 1 inch apart as they will rise a lot when baked. Repeat with the remaining dough, working in batches depending on how many baking sheets you have.

7. In a small bowl, combine the egg yolks and water and whisk with a fork. Brush the tops of the koulourakia and bake for 15 minutes, until nice and golden!

8. Let the koulourakia cool completely on a wire rack and store in an airtight container for up to three weeks.

NUTRITION DATA FOR 1 SERVING (2 COOKIES):

Calories **88kcal**	Sodium **47mg**
Total Carbohydrates **14g**	Potassium **28mg**
Protein **2g**	Dietary Fiber **1g**
Total Fat **3g**	Sugars **4g**
Saturated Fat **2g**	Vitamin A **7% Daily Value**
Polyunsaturated Fat **1g**	Vitamin C **12% Daily Value**
Monounsaturated Fat **1g**	Calcium **27% Daily Value**
Trans Fat **0.1g**	Iron **13% Daily Value**
Cholesterol **28mg**	

Makes: 8

The perfect substitute for when you have that craving for ice cream! You can even eat this one every night to top up your Calcium and Iron intake.

Frozen Blueberry Yogurt Swirl Pop Cups

INGREDIENTS

2 cups blueberries

2 cups Greek yogurt

2 tbsp. agave or honey

1 drop liquid stevia

8 wooden craft sticks

INSTRUCTIONS

Blend the blueberries in a food processor or blender until they're smoothie-like in consistency. Pour into a bowl and gently mix in the yogurt, agave or honey and stevia. Pour the mixture into an 8-popsicle mold and insert the wooden craft sticks. Freeze for at least 5 hours. When ready to serve, run under warm water to get the popsicles out of the mold.

NUTRITION DATA FOR 1 SERVING:

Calories **120kcal**
Total Carbohydrates **18g**
Protein **4g**
Total Fat **4g**
Saturated Fat **2g**
Polyunsaturated Fat **1g**
Monounsaturated Fat **1g**
Trans Fat **1g**
Cholesterol **15mg**
Sodium **85mg**
Potassium **41mg**
Dietary Fiber **0g**
Sugars **2g**
Vitamin A **2.6% Daily Value**
Vitamin C **3.4% Daily Value**
Calcium **6.4% Daily Value**
Iron **7% Daily Value**

Serves: 8

One of my personal favorites for a late night snack, with 18g of protein and 21mg of Potassium it will be sure to satisfy!

Frozen Chocolate Bananas

INGREDIENTS

4 bananas

8 wooden craft sticks

⅓ cup almond butter

¼ cup dark chocolate

½ cup almonds, chopped

INSTRUCTIONS

1. Cut bananas in half. Insert a wooden craft stick into the bottom of each banana. Freeze the bananas on parchment-lined baking sheet for about 3 hours.

2. Spread the almond butter over each banana, then freeze for another hour.

3. Melt the chocolate in the top of a double boiler. Dip each banana into the chocolate. Spread the chopped almonds out on a plate and roll the chocolate-dipped bananas over the almonds to coat. Freeze again until the chocolate is firm, another 1–2 hours.

Tip: substitute cashews or walnuts for the almonds.

NUTRITION DATA FOR 1 SERVING:

Calories **100kcal**	Sodium **7mg**
Total Carbohydrates **39g**	Potassium **21mg**
Protein **18g**	Dietary Fiber **2g**
Total Fat **6g**	Sugars **1g**
Saturated Fat **3g**	Vitamin A **4% Daily Value**
Polyunsaturated Fat **1g**	Vitamin C **7.1% Daily Value**
Monounsaturated Fat **2g**	Calcium **6% Daily Value**
Trans Fat **1g**	Iron**13% Daily Value**
Cholesterol **0mg**	

Chocolate Chia Pudding with Raspberries

Serves: 4

Looking for a light snack high in Potassium? This Dark Chocolate Chia Pudding is just that!

INGREDIENTS

1½ cups almond milk

¼ cup dark chocolate chips

3 tbsp. chia seeds

¼ cup raspberries

¼ cup almonds

8 mint leaves (optional)

INSTRUCTIONS

Combine 1 cup of the almond milk and the chocolate chips in a pot over low heat. Stir to melt the chocolate slowly, making sure not to scald the milk. Stir in the remaining milk and let cool to room temperature. Pour the chocolate mixture into 4 serving glasses glass and fold in the chia seeds. Let stand for 15 minutes, then stir again. Cover and transfer to the refrigerator for at least 8 hours. When ready to serve, stir the chia seed mixture and top with the raspberries, almonds and mint leaves, if using.

NUTRITION DATA FOR 1 SERVING:

Calories **220kcal**	Sodium **90mg**
Total Carbohydrates **28g**	Potassium **81mg**
Protein **6g**	Dietary Fiber **2g**
Total Fat **11g**	Sugars **3g**
Saturated Fat **3g**	Vitamin A **3% Daily Value**
Polyunsaturated Fat **4g**	Vitamin C **4.6% Daily Value**
Monounsaturated Fat **2g**	Calcium **2.6% Daily Value**
Trans Fat **2g**	Iron **8% Daily Value**
Cholesterol **35mg**	

Serves: 2

Chia Seed Pudding is always a great choice! There are so many different fruits that go so well with it and its such a great late night snack.

Chia Seed & Mango Purée with Blueberries

INGREDIENTS

¼ cup chia seeds

1½ cups almond milk

1 tbsp. honey or agave

½ tsp. vanilla extract

1 drop liquid stevia

1 mango, peeled and pit removed

½ cup blueberries

2 mint leaves

INSTRUCTIONS

Mix the chia seeds, almond milk, honey or agave, vanilla extract and stevia in a bowl until combined. Allow the chia seed mixture to soak for 2 hours in the refrigerator. Purée the mango in a food processor or blender. Fold the mango purée into the chia seed mixture. Divide between two serving dishes and garnish with the blueberries and mint.

NUTRITION DATA FOR 1 SERVING:

Calories **341kcal**
Total Carbohydrates **44g**
Protein **14g**
Total Fat **28g**
Saturated Fat **14g**
Polyunsaturated Fat **6g**
Monounsaturated Fat **8g**
Trans Fat **0g**
Cholesterol **0mg**
Sodium **141mg**
Potassium **76mg**
Dietary Fiber **19g**
Sugars **34g**
Vitamin A **6% Daily Value**
Vitamin C **11% Daily Value**
Calcium **24% Daily Value**
Iron **15% Daily Value**

Serves: 2

Where sweet and savoury meet on a plate. This unique recipe is will change the way you see Pears and will keep you coming back for more!

Caramelized Pear with Gorgonzola

INGREDIENTS

2 tbsp. olive oil

1 ripe pear, cored and sliced

¼ cup gorgonzola cheese

¼ cup Natural Caramel Sauce (recipe follows)

3 tbsp. honey or agave

alfalfa sprouts (optional)

INSTRUCTIONS

Heat the olive oil in a pan over medium heat. Add the pear and cook until lightly browned, about 5–7 minutes. Add the gorgonzola cheese, gently stir and continue cooking until the cheese begins to melt, about 3–5 minutes. Divide the pear slices between 2 plates and garnish with the caramel sauce, honey and sprouts, if using.

NUTRITION DATA FOR 1 SERVING:

Calories **260kcal**	Sodium **31mg**
Total Carbohydrates **39g**	Potassium **23mg**
Protein **22g**	Dietary Fiber **4g**
Total Fat **18g**	Sugars **14g**
Saturated Fat **5g**	Vitamin A **4% Daily Value**
Polyunsaturated Fat **11g**	Vitamin C **14% Daily Value**
Monounsaturated Fat **2g**	Calcium **16% Daily Value**
Trans Fat **0g**	Iron **11% Daily Value**
Cholesterol **0mg**	

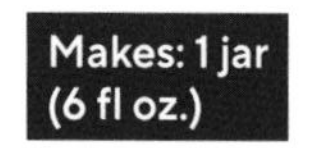
Makes: 1 jar (6 fl oz.)

Natural Carmel Sauce is always something I have on hand! It holds well and compliments all those amazing fruit dishes that might need just a little extra zing!

Natural Caramel Sauce

INGREDIENTS

¼ cup plus 2 tbsp. powdered erythritol

¼ cup water

2 tbsp. maple syrup

¼ cup butter

⅓ cup heavy cream

INSTRUCTIONS

Combine the erythritol, water and maple syrup in a medium saucepan over medium heat and bring to a boil. Add the butter and whisk for about 10 minutes until the mixture begins to brown. Turn off the heat and add in the cream. Turn the heat to medium-high and whisk for 2 minutes. Once the sauce begins to thicken and reaches the consistency of caramel sauce, turn off the heat completely. Serve immediately, or transfer to a jar and store for up to 1 week.

NUTRITION DATA FOR 1 SERVING:

Calories **80kcal**	Sodium **65mg**
Total Carbohydrates **39g**	Potassium **25mg**
Protein **11g**	Dietary Fiber **2g**
Total Fat **3g**	Sugars **0g**
Saturated Fat **1g**	Vitamin A **3% Daily Value**
Polyunsaturated Fat **1g**	Vitamin C **7% Daily Value**
Monounsaturated Fat **1g**	Calcium **15% Daily Value**
Trans Fat **0g**	Iron **5% Daily Value**
Cholesterol **0mg**	

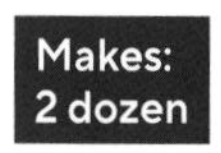

Who said cookies can't be healthy? 24% of your daily Calcium, 16% of your daily Iron! Just make sure you don't eat them all in one night.

Chocolate Chip Cookies

INGREDIENTS

2½ cups Swerve sugar replacement

1 cup olive oil

1 tbsp. vanilla extract

1 tsp. salt

1 large egg

2 cups flour

½ tsp. baking soda

2 cups unsweetened chocolate chips

INSTRUCTIONS

1. Preheat the oven to 350°F and line two baking sheets with parchment paper.

2. Combine the Swerve, oil, vanilla extract and salt in a large bowl and mix until smooth. Mix in the egg. In a separate bowl, combine the flour and baking soda. Combine the wet and dry ingredients, then fold in the chocolate chips.

3. Form the dough into 1-inch balls and place them on the prepared baking sheets, pressing down slightly and leaving 1 inch between the cookies to allow them to expand.

4. Bake until the cookies are golden brown around the edges, about 10 minutes. Cool on a rack before serving.

NUTRITION DATA FOR 1 SERVING (4 COOKIES):

Calories **400kcal**	Sodium **214mg**
Total Carbohydrates **58g**	Potassium **135mg**
Protein **6g**	Dietary Fiber **5g**
Total Fat **29g**	Sugars **2g**
Saturated Fat **14g**	Vitamin A **6% Daily Value**
Polyunsaturated Fat **5g**	Vitamin C **5.7% Daily Value**
Monounsaturated Fat **8g**	Calcium **24% Daily Value**
Trans Fat **0g**	Iron **16% Daily Value**
Cholesterol **70mg**	

Lemon Bars with Tahini Crust

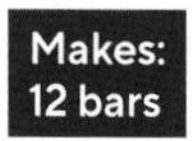

Makes: 12 bars

I just love the sweet flavor of lemon for dessert! This one has such a beautiful crisp crust and just enough lemon to push through the tofu!

INGREDIENTS

FOR THE TAHINI CRUST:

½ cup rolled oats

½ cup sesame seeds

8 dates

¼ cup tahini

¼ tsp. salt

FOR THE LEMON FILLING:

1 cup fresh lemon juice

14 oz. firm tofu

¼ cup plus 1 tbsp. Swerve sugar replacement

1 tbsp. arrowroot starch

¼ tbsp. lemon zest

INSTRUCTIONS

1. Preheat the oven to 350°F and line an 8-inch baking dish with parchment paper.

2. Combine the oats and sesame seeds in the bowl of a food processor and pulse for 30 seconds. Add the dates, tahini and salt and blend until combined, about 90 seconds. Press the mixture down into the prepared baking dish until evenly distributed. Press to pack it down. Bake until the edges are golden brown, about 15 minutes.

3. Combine the lemon juice, tofu, Swerve, arrowroot starch and lemon zest in food processor until smooth. Pour onto the baked crust and bake for an additional 35 minutes. Let cool, then refrigerate for about 90 minutes until the custard is set. Cut into 12 squares and lift out, using the parchment paper.

NUTRITION DATA FOR 1 SERVING (1 BAR):

Calories **189kcal**
Total Carbohydrates **15g**
Protein **7g**
Total Fat **6g**
Saturated Fat **3g**
Polyunsaturated Fat **1g**
Monounsaturated Fat **1g**
Trans Fat **1g**
Cholesterol **0mg**
Sodium **45mg**
Potassium **41mg**
Dietary Fiber **2g**
Sugars **0g**
Vitamin A **3% Daily Value**
Vitamin C **8.3% Daily Value**
Calcium **4.6% Daily Value**
Iron **12% Daily Value**

Serves: 6

There's nothing quite like a smooth Pistachio Pudding. Very tart, amazing texture and a sweetness that just seems to always find it's way through!

Pistachio Pudding

INGREDIENTS

1 cup shelled unsalted pistachios, plus more for garnish

½ cup Swerve sugar replacement

2 cups plus 2 tbsp. almond milk

1 egg, plus 2 egg yolks

2 tbsp. maple syrup

dash of salt

2 tbsp. olive oil

¼ tbsp. vanilla extract

INSTRUCTIONS

1. Blend the pistachios in a food processor until finely ground. Add ¼ cup of the Swerve and 2 tablespoons of the almond milk. Pulse until a paste forms. Transfer the paste to a saucepan and add the remaining 2 cups of almond milk. Cook over medium-high heat until the mixture begins to steam.

2. Meanwhile, in the food processor, blend the remaining ¼ cup of Swerve with the whole egg, egg yolks, maple syrup and salt. With the processor still running, slowly add ½ cup of the warm milk mixture to temper the eggs so that the mixture does not curdle.

3. Slowly add the contents of the food processor back into the pan with the milk mixture and continue to cook. Reduce the heat to medium and cook until the pudding begins to bubble and thicken, about 6–8 minutes. Remove from the heat and add the oil and vanilla. Divide into 6 serving cups, and chill for at least 4 hours or overnight. Serve cold, garnished with chopped pistachios.

NUTRITION DATA FOR 1 SERVING:

Calories **100kcal**	Monounsaturated Fat **0.1g**	Sugars **2g**
Total Carbohydrates **24g**	Trans Fat **0g**	Vitamin A **7% Daily Value**
Protein **1g**	Cholesterol **0mg**	Vitamin C **5% Daily Value**
Total Fat **1g**	Sodium **90mg**	Calcium **8% Daily Value**
Saturated Fat **1g**	Potassium **37mg**	Iron **4% Daily Value**
Polyunsaturated Fat **1g**	Dietary Fiber **1g**	

Index

JOURNAL

JOURNAL

JOURNAL

JOURNAL